Collaborative Strategic Reading

Strategies for Improving Comprehension

Janette K. Klingner, Ph.D. ✳ Sharon Vaughn, Ph.D.

Joseph Dimino, Ph.D. ✳ Jeanne S. Schumm, Ph.D. ✳ Diane Bryant, Ph.D.

Edited by Mitchell Duval
Cover/Text design by Sherri Rowe
Cover illustration by Steve Clark
Production assistance by Kimberly Harris

ISBN 1-57035-452-9

Printed in the United States of America

Published and Distributed by

SOPRIS
WEST
EDUCATIONAL SERVICES

A Cambium Learning™ Company

4093 Specialty Place • Longmont, CO 80504
(303) 651-2829 • www.**sopriswest**.com

150READ/3-05

Acknowledgments

We offer our sincere gratitude to the many teachers who have used CSR in their classrooms over the years and who helped us with its development. In particular, we would like to thank Tiffany Royal and Joyce Duryea for their many contributions. We would like to thank the principals, Kathy Astley and Kathy Caballero, and teachers at Flamingo and Kensington Park Elementary Schools in Miami-Dade County for their school-wide implementation of CSR. We would also like to thank Greg Sherry in Oregon, and the sixth- and seventh-grade teachers at Webb Middle School in Austin for teaching us so much about integrating reading comprehension instruction into content area teaching. Finally, we would like to thank Ae-hwa Kim for working to make CSR available through technology.

Contents

Introduction

What is Collaborative Strategic Reading? An Overview

Mrs. Garcia is a fourth-grade teacher who was concerned about the reading performance of her students. Most of them could read the words, but they often didn't seem to understand what they read. Mrs. Garcia was particularly worried that they were not able to tell the main idea of the text after they read it. She was also worried about their performance on the state-wide assessment test in reading that would be given in the spring. She had spent considerable time asking her students questions, encouraging them to reread text to put together answers, and reinforcing students who seemed to interpret the text well. But she was still very worried that the majority of her students were not making suitable progress in reading comprehension. Of further concern was the fact that her students had difficulty comprehending narrative text but even more difficulty with expository text. Mrs. Garcia realized that her students needed to learn to understand what they read in both text types.

With concerns like those expressed by Mrs. Garcia in mind, we have worked over the last ten years to design an instructional practice that would improve reading comprehension of both

Chapter at a Glance

- **Overview of Collaborative Strategic Reading (CSR)**
  1. Preview
  2. Click and Clunk
  3. Get the Gist
  4. Wrap Up

- **Why Teach CSR?**

- **What Research Supports CSR?**

- **A Note About CSR and Content Area Instruction**

- **How is the Rest of the Book Organized?**

expository and narrative texts and that could be implemented effectively by teachers. We were interested in designing an intervention practice that would use what we know about effective reading comprehension as well as what we know about effective student engagement and learning. In formulating our approach, we were also sensitive to the realities of classroom teachers and their concerns.

Collaborative Strategic Reading (CSR) combines the essential reading comprehension strategies that have been demonstrated to be effective in improving students' understanding of text (Palincsar & Brown, 1984; Rosenshine & Meister, 1994) with cooperative learning groups or paired learning (Johnson & Johnson, 1989; Kagan, 1986). CSR takes advantage of the growing knowledge among educators that youngsters need to be taught specific strategies to enhance their understanding of a text but should not be overwhelmed with so many strategies that they are unable to decide which ones to use.

Following is a brief description of the four reading strategies taught within CSR: Preview, Click and Clunk, Get the Gist, and Wrap Up. These strategies and their applications will be explained in more depth in Chapters 2 and 3.

Preview

Students implement the "Preview" strategy *before* reading the day's text passage, by scanning the material and searching for clues. The purpose of the Preview strategy is to activate background knowledge and to generate informed predictions about the text to be read. The primary goals of previewing are to:

* Generate interest in the text

* Stimulate background knowledge and associations with the text

* Provide an opportunity to make informed predictions about what will be learned from reading the text

* Encourage active reading of the text

The Preview strategy has two steps. The first of these is *brainstorming*. When students brainstorm, they think about and discuss what they have already learned about the topic, perhaps in previous lessons or from friends, relatives, or teachers, or maybe from reading or watching a television program about the topic. The second step is *predicting*. Predicting involves finding clues in the title, subheadings, pictures, and content of a passage that might suggest what the text will be about. Students are provided a very short time (two to three minutes) to preview the text passage. They then take five to seven minutes to write what they already know about the subject and what they predict they will learn, and to discuss their previews. Remember that previewing, like all of the strategies taught within CSR, is a strategy that can be used throughout the day and across the curriculum.

Click and Clunk

Whereas previewing is a strategy used prior to reading, "Click and Clunk" is a self-monitoring strategy that is implemented *during* reading. The purposes of Click and Clunk are to teach students: (a) the metacognitive, or self-learning, skills to monitor their own comprehension; and (b) a method of figuring out the meanings of challenging words or concepts. When students are reading and everything "clicks," they understand the content of what they are reading. They recognize material they know a lot about. On the other hand, students encounter "clunks" when their comprehension breaks down. Clunks are words or concepts that they don't understand and need to know more about in order to comprehend what they are reading and learning. After reading a paragraph or section of the text, students stop reading momentarily to identify and figure out their clunks. Students learn to "declunk" words by seeking help from their peers and by using "fix-up" strategies. These fix-up strategies direct students to:

1. Reread the sentence with the clunk and look for key ideas to help them figure out the word. They think about what makes sense.

2. Read the sentences before and after the clunks to look for clues.

3. Look for a prefix or suffix that might help.

4. Break the word apart into smaller words that they know.

These fix-up strategies are written on "clunk cards" that assist students in "declunking" words. Sample clunk cards are pictured in the Materials section of this book (Chapter 4). When no one in a CSR group can figure out what a clunk means, students are taught to ask the teacher. However, they are instructed to keep reading rather than waiting until the teacher can come to their assistance. Many teachers believe that this is the most valuable aspect of CSR. They notice that their students internalize these Click and Clunk strategies and are able to apply them in different contexts, including on high stakes tests. It is not uncommon, the teachers report, to hear students in the library or lunchroom, wherever they are reading, say to each other, "Hey, do you know the meaning of this clunk word?"

Get the Gist

Like the Click and Clunk strategy, students "Get the Gist" while they are reading, stopping after every paragraph or section of text to implement the strategies. Depending upon the length of a passage, students may stop to Click and Clunk and Get the Gist from three to five times during one CSR session. The purpose of Get the Gist is to teach students to identify the most critical information in the paragraph or section of text they have just read, in other words, to determine the main idea. The "main idea" is frequently touted as an important reading comprehension skill, and while many teachers ask students to tell them the main idea, few actually teach the steps needed to do so. In CSR, students are taught first to name the most important "who" or "what" in the section of text they have just read and then to identify the most important information about the "who" or "what," rephrasing the main idea in their own

words. Some teachers ask students to limit their responses to ten words or less (Fuchs, Fuchs, Mathes, & Simmons, 1997). The intent is to assist students in providing the "gist" of a text in as few words as possible while also conveying the essential meaning and excluding unnecessary details.

Wrap Up

"Wrap Up," like Preview, occurs only once during the strategic reading process, but, unlike Preview, it comes *after* reading the day's selection. The purpose of Wrap Up is to teach students to identify the most significant ideas in the entire passage they've read and then to assist them with understanding and remembering what they've learned. Wrap Up includes two steps: (a) generating and answering questions about the passage, and (b) reviewing what was learned.

Students *generate questions* concerning what they have read by thinking about the important ideas in the passage and then forming the questions that a good teacher might ask students to see if they really understand the material. Students are encouraged to think of questions that might be asked on a test. They start their questions with "the five W's and an H" (who, what, when, where, why, and how). Some questions should be about information stated explicitly in the passage and other questions should require an answer not right in the passage but "in your head." This type of question asks for an opinion and can have more than one right answer. Students are encouraged to ask questions that involve higher-level thinking skills rather than literal recall. Some teachers provide their students with question stems (adapted from Rosenshine & Meister, 1992):

* How were _____ and _____ the same? Different?

* What do you think would happen if _____?

* What do you think caused _____ to happen?

* How would you compare and contrast
  _____?

* What might have prevented the problem of
  _____ from happening?

* What are the strengths and weaknesses of
  _____?

After students have constructed one or two questions, they take turns asking their classmates to answer their "best" questions.

To implement the second step of Wrap Up, *review*, students write down the most important ideas they learned from the day's reading assignment in their CSR learning logs. The review strategy requires students to mentally organize textual information and to focus on comprehension of the text as a whole. This increases understanding and memory of text. Students take turns sharing what they learned with their groups and perhaps the whole class. Many students can share their "best idea" in a short period of time, providing the teacher with valuable information about each student's level of understanding.

In summary, students "Preview" the day's reading assignment (e.g., a section of the social studies textbook) by asking each other what they already know about the topic and what they predict they will learn. After reading a short segment of text, students "Click and Clunk" by making sure everyone in the group understands key vocabulary in the text. Next, students "Get the Gist" by figuring out the main idea of the paragraph or section they have just read. They "Click and Clunk" and "Get the Gist" as they read each short section of text. Finally, after they have finished all of the day's reading, students "Wrap Up" by restating the most important information learned that day and formulating questions they think the teacher might ask on a test. *CSR's Plan for Strategic Reading* illustrates this sequence (**Figure 1-1**).

Collaborative Strategic Reading might seem complicated at first. However, most teachers already implement comprehension strategies and cooperative learning to some degree. CSR puts these practices together in a way that is manageable.

We recommend introducing CSR in *two* stages. During Stage One, the teacher presents the strategies to the whole class using "think-alouds," modeling, and role playing. Students practice the strategies for several days, with text, developing their skills. Once the students use the strategies proficiently, they are ready to move to Stage Two. During the second stage, students learn the roles that they will use in their cooperative learning groups. Then they can be divided into small groups of four or five students to implement CSR with minimal adult assistance.

Why Teach CSR?

What are the goals of CSR?

The goals of CSR are to improve students' reading comprehension and increase their conceptual learning. CSR procedures are designed to maximize students' involvement and help all students to be successful in heterogeneous, or mixed learning level, classrooms.

Why should we teach comprehension strategies?

Comprehension strategies reflect the mental processes or tactics used by successful readers when interacting with text. As students progress through the elementary grades, they are required to read increasingly complex levels of material in content area textbooks. Reading comprehension plays a larger and larger role as students mature. Comprehension strategy instruction is based on the premise that even students who have difficulty understanding text can be successfully taught to apply the strategies used by good readers, and that when poor readers learn to apply these strategies, their reading comprehension will improve. Comprehension strategies are helpful for *all* readers, but are *critical* for students with learning problems.

Figure 1-1

CSR's Plan for Strategic Reading

Before Reading

Preview

1. BRAINSTORM — What do we already know about the topic?

2. PREDICT — What do we predict we will learn about the topic when we read the passage?

During Reading

Click and Clunk

1. Were there any parts that were hard to understand (clunks)?

2. How can we fix the clunks? Use fix-up strategies:
   (a) Reread the sentence with the clunk and look for key ideas to help you understand.
   (b) Reread the sentences before and after the clunk to look for clues.
   (c) Look for a prefix or suffix in the word.
   (d) Break the word apart and look for smaller words.

Get the Gist

1. What is the most important person, place, or thing in this section?

2. What is the most important idea about the person, place, or thing?

After Reading

Wrap Up

1. ASK QUESTIONS — What questions check whether we understand the most important information in the passage? Can we answer the questions?

2. REVIEW — What did we learn?

Why should we include cooperative learning?

In comparison with competitive or individualized methods, cooperative learning has been found to improve academic performance, lead to greater motivation towards learning, increase time on task, improve self-esteem, and lead to more positive social behaviors. Cooperative learning fosters the development of higher level reasoning and problem solving skills. Cooperative learning is effective in diverse classrooms that include a wide range of achievement levels, and has been recommended by experts in the fields of multicultural education, English as a second language (ESL), special education, and general education.

Why do we need Collaborative Strategic Reading?

Many teachers have told us that they want to teach comprehension strategies and help students improve their ability to learn from text but have not been able to find a method that is feasible with large classes. CSR provides a systematic, practical procedure for teaching comprehension strategies to an entire class of students with a range of reading abilities. When the Miami-Dade County Public Schools (M-DCPS) Language Arts Director observed CSR implemented in a fourth-grade classroom for the first time, she became very excited. She said, "You have worked out all the kinks. Reciprocal Teaching, as great as it is, just seemed too challenging to implement with an entire class. But you've figured out how to make it work. I love it. If the superintendent were to say that starting tomorrow every teacher in M-DCPS would have to implement CSR in order to keep their job in this district, I would jump up and down and shout 'hallelujah'!"

How is CSR different than Reciprocal Teaching?

While working with administrators, reading leaders, and teachers across the country, we are sometimes asked how CSR differs from Reciprocal Teaching. After all, both are methods for implementing reading comprehension strategies. CSR is, in fact, an outgrowth of Reciprocal Teaching. After implementing Reciprocal Teaching in our earlier work (Klingner & Vaughn, 1996), we adapted the method until we had made so many changes that we felt we had come up with an instructional approach sufficiently different to warrant a new name. **Table 1-1** illustrates the differences between the two methods.

What Research Supports the Use of CSR?

We designed CSR to capitalize on the best research-based elements devised to enhance reading comprehension and content learning. Our goal was to develop a model that would be effective in diverse classrooms that include students with reading disabilities. CSR has been implemented successfully in classrooms from third grade through middle school.

Research validates the effectiveness of the comprehension strategies and cooperative learning approaches that were combined to form CSR, as well as CSR itself. Comprehension strategy instruction has improved learning opportunities for students with learning disabilities (LD) (for reviews see Pressley, Brown, El-Dinary, & Afflerbach, 1995; Weisberg, 1988) and limited-English-proficient (LEP) students (Anderson & Roit, 1996; Chamot & O'Malley, 1996; Hernandez, 1991; Klingner & Vaughn, 1996). Cooperative learning has also produced favorable results for students with LD (e.g., Madden & Slavin, 1983; Stevens & Slavin, 1995) and ESL students (e.g., Durán & Szymanski, 1995; Jacob, Rottenberg, Patrick, & Wheeler, 1996; Long & Porter, 1985). And it's been shown that this type of peer interaction increases opportunities for meaningful communication about academic content (Cazden, 1988; Richard-Amato, 1992).

Table 1-1

How CSR and Reciprocal Teaching Differ

Reciprocal Teaching	Collaborative Strategic Reading
Designed primarily for use with narrative text.	Designed primarily for use with expository text.
No **brainstorming** before reading.	Students **brainstorm** to activate prior knowledge as part of **preview** (before reading).
Students predict what they think will happen next before reading each paragraph or segment of text.	Students only **predict** as part of the Preview strategy (before reading), making informed guesses about what they think they will learn.
Students **clarify** words or chunks of text they don't understand by rereading the sentences before and after the sentence they don't understand, and/or asking a peer for assistance.	Students use "fix-up strategies" to clarify "**clunks**" (words they don't understand): – Reread the sentence. – Reread the sentences before and after. – Break apart the work and look for smaller words they know. – Look for a prefix or suffix they know. – Look at the picture for clues. – Ask for help.
Students **summarize** the paragraph or segment of text they have just read.	Students **get the gist** of the paragraph or segment of text they have just read, identifying "the most important who or what" and the most important information about the who or what. They then say the gist in ten words or less.
Students **generate questions** after each paragraph or segment of text they have just read.	Students only **generate questions** as part of a **wrap up** after they have read the entire day's selection. Students answer each other's questions.
No **review** after reading.	Students **review** what they have learned after reading the day's selection.
8–12 students in the group; the teacher in the group.	An entire class is divided into **cooperative groups** of 2–5; the teacher circulates rather than staying with a group.
No learning logs.	Students record their previews, clunks, questions, and what they've learned in individual **CSR Learning Logs**.
The "leader" (a student) facilitates the discussion about a paragraph or section of text; this role rotates after each paragraph.	Every student in the group has a meaningful role; one of these roles is to be the "leader." Roles are assigned for an entire lesson (only rotating biweekly in some classes).
No cue cards.	Students use **Cue Cards** to help them implement their roles and the comprehension strategies.

Investigations of CSR's effectiveness have consistently yielded positive results. A brief review of CSR studies and a summary of CSR effect sizes follow. Some of these studies were conducted in Florida and others in Texas.

In our first investigation of CSR (Klingner, Vaughn, & Schumm, 1998), we taught 85 fourth graders to apply CSR comprehension strategies while reading social studies text in small student-led groups. Fifty-six students in comparison classrooms did not learn the comprehension strategies but received teacher-led instruction in the same content for the same period of time (11 sessions that lasted 45 minutes each). We found that students who used CSR made greater gains on the Gates-MacGinitie Reading Comprehension Test than students who did not, and that they made equal gains in content knowledge. We tape recorded and transcribed students' conversations while they worked in their cooperative learning groups and found that, for the most part, students were able to implement the CSR strategies while working collaboratively. We concluded that, overall, CSR appeared to be feasible for use in general education elementary classrooms with heterogeneous populations. However, we also learned valuable lessons that we then applied in our subsequent efforts to "fine-tune" CSR.

In our next study, we investigated the frequency and means with which bilingual students helped each other and their limited-English-proficient peers while working in small, heterogeneous CSR groups (Klingner & Vaughn, 2000). Given the changes made in CSR since our previous study, we wanted to determine the ways that students helped each other learn new vocabulary words. We also expected to find that students would spend a greater percentage of time engaged in academic discussion, particularly in comparison with the fourth graders in our previous study. We found that, overall, students spent nearly all of their time engaged in academic-related strategic discussion and almost no time (less than one percent) engaged in procedural negotiation. Students assisted one another in understanding word meanings, getting the main

idea, asking and answering questions, and relating previous knowledge to what they were learning. Students' scores on English vocabulary tests improved significantly from pre- to posttest.

In a more recent investigation, we compared student outcomes in five fourth-grade classrooms where CSR was implemented with five classrooms where it was not (Klingner, Vaughn, Arguelles, Hughes, & Ahwee, 2001). This was the first study in which classroom teachers implemented CSR with minimal assistance from us (other than initial training and ongoing monitoring) and student outcomes were compared with matched control classrooms. The challenges experienced by the teachers who implemented CSR were documented to help us better understand and facilitate future instruction. We found that CSR students gained more than comparison students on the Gates-MacGinitie Reading Comprehension Test. Low achieving students in CSR classes showed the greatest gains. In general, those CSR teachers with higher levels of CSR implementation (in quantity and quality) yielded greater gains in comprehension than those CSR teachers with lower levels of implementation.

In another investigation, this time in Texas, we studied both the integration of CSR into middle school instructional teams and the role of peer-mediated strategies in improving academic outcomes (Bryant, Vaughn et al., 1999). The purpose of this study was to describe the reading outcomes of a multi-component intervention on the fluency, word identification, and comprehension abilities of average-achieving middle school students, low-achieving students, and students with learning disabilities. Ten sixth-grade middle school teachers participated in a six month professional development and intervention program to enhance reading outcomes. Teachers were taught CSR during an all-day workshop and provided with materials, time as a team to develop an implementation plan, and in-class follow-up support. Overall, all three groups of students improved in oral reading accuracy and fluency, and significant student gains in word identification, fluency, and comprehension were noted. However, a subgroup of very poor readers made little or no gains in reading achievement across the three interventions.

We next conducted a follow-up study that focused on CSR as a reading comprehension strategy that could be implemented by middle school teachers across content area classes (Bryant, Ugel, Hougen, Hamff, & Vaughn, 1999). A team of six seventh-grade teachers participated in a year-long study that focused on the implementation of CSR into content reading instruction for average-achieving students, low-achieving students, and students with learning disabilities in reading. Teachers were asked to incorporate CSR into their instruction two to three times weekly, and to attend weekly support group meetings. Teachers were also asked to implement the peer-mediated component of CSR in a manner that worked best for them and their students. Preliminary overall findings suggest that CSR enhanced reading outcomes.

Table 1-2 lists the CSR studies described above and presents the effect sizes associated with each. The authors of the study and the type of comparison reported are provided in the first column. The student achievement group(s) for whom effect sizes are reported are listed in the second. The outcome measures used in the study are listed in the third column; the effect size for each outcome is provided separately in the fourth, and then mean effect sizes are listed in the fifth (Kim, 2000). All of the effect sizes in the fourth column were included in calculating the mean effect sizes provided in the last column.

A Note about CSR and Content Area Instruction

As many teachers are aware, content area instruction requires a variety of instructional modes, including experimentation, research, and inquiry, to name just a few. CSR is not intended to be the only form of content area instruction a teacher uses for a science or social studies unit. We think that CSR is an excellent tool to supplement or replace whole class read-the-chapter-and-answer-the-questions activities. But CSR should not replace other activities associated with effective content area instruction such as hands on projects, experiments, inquiry-based learning, and other types of content area work.

How is the Rest of the Book Organized?

The chapter you have just read provided an overview of Collaborative Strategic Reading. It included a description of the purpose, the critical components of the instructional practice, when and how it has been used in the past, and a description of the research and effect sizes that support its use and implementation. We hope that you are now motivated to learn more about CSR and how you might implement it in your classroom.

The next chapter will address how to teach the CSR comprehension strategies, and then there is a chapter providing information about cooperative learning. The fourth chapter will present materials related to the implementation of CSR. The fifth chapter is geared toward assisting secondary teachers in implementing CSR.

Table 1-2

Effect Sizes for Learning Disabled and Low-Achieving Students in CSR Studies

Authors	Targeted Students	Measure	Effect Size	Mean Effect Size
Klingner & Vaughn (1996; pre vs. post)				
	LD	Gates-MacGinitie Reading Test (Comprehension) for tutoring	0.54	0.91
		Passage comprehension tests for tutoring	1.31	
		Strategy interview for tutoring	1.25	
		Gates-MacGinitie Reading Test (Comprehension) for cooperative learning	0.55	
		Passage comprehension tests for cooperative learning	0.88	
		Strategy interview for cooperative learning	0.91	
Klingner, Vaughn, & Schumm (1998; treatment vs. control)				
	LD, LA, AA, & HA (combined)	Gates-MacGinitie Reading Test (Comprehension)	0.44	0.28
		Content measure	0.12	
*Klingner, Vaughn, Hughes, Schumm, & Elbaum (1998; pre vs. post)				
	LD	Basic Academic Skills Samples—Reading	0.78	0.78
Klingner & Vaughn (2000; pre vs. post)				
	LA	Vocabulary test for Chapter 14	1.33	1.50
		Vocabulary test for Chapter 15	1.66	

Table 1-2 (continued)

Effect Sizes for Learning Disabled and Low-Achieving Students in CSR Studies

Authors	Targeted Students	Measure	Effect Size	Mean Effect Size
Klingner, Vaughn, Arguelles, Hughes, & Ahwee (2000; pre vs. post)				
	LD & LA	Gates-MacGinitie Reading Test (Comprehension)	0.42 (LD) 1.40 (LA)	0.98 (LD) 1.67 (LA)
		Social Studies Content Test	1.35 (LD) 1.94 (LA)	
		Vocabulary Test	1.16 (LD) 1.67 (LA)	
*Bryant, Vaughn, Linan-Thompson, Ugel, Hamff, & Hougen (2000; pre vs. post)				
	LD	Reading comprehension test	0.22	0.51
		Test of Oral Rdg. Fluency	0.67	
		Word identification strategy verbal practice checklist	0.64	
Vaughn, Chard, Bryant, Coleman, Tyler, Thompson, & Kouzekanani (2000; pre vs. post)				
	LD	Gray Oral Reading Test – 3 (GORT) – Rate	0.35	0.33
		GORT – Accuracy	0.03	
		GORT – Comprehension	0.16	
		Correct Words Per Minute	1.18	

Note

Pre = pretest
Post = posttest
LD = students with learning disabilities
LA = low-achieving students
AA = average achieving students
HA = high achieving

* These were multicomponent interventions in which CSR was one of the featured interventions.

References

Anderson, V., & M. Roit. (1996). Linking reading comprehension instruction to language development for language-minority students. *The Elementary School Journal, 96,* 295–309.

Bryant, D. P., S. Vaughn, S. Linan-Thompson, N. Ugel, & A. Hamff. (2000). Reading outcomes for students with and without learning disabilities in general education middle school content area classes. *Learning Disability Quarterly, 23*(3), 24–38.

Bryant, D. P., N. Ugel, M. Hougen, A. Hamff, & S. Vaughn. (1999). *The effects of Collaborative Strategic Reading on reading outcomes of seventh grade students with learning disabilities in general education classrooms.* Unpublished manuscript.

Cazden, C. B. (1988). *Classroom discourse: The language of teaching and learning.* Portsmouth, NH: Heinemann.

Chamot, A. U., & J. M. O'Malley. (1996). The Cognitive Academic Language Learning Approach: A model for linguistically diverse classrooms. *The Elementary School Journal, 96,* 259–273.

Durán, R. P., & M. H. Szymanski. (1995). Cooperative learning interaction and construction of activity. *Discourse Processes, 19,* 149–169.

Fuchs, D., L. S. Fuchs, P. Mathes, & D. Simmons. (1997). Peer-assisted learning strategies: Making classrooms more responsive to student diversity. *American Educational Research Journal, 34,* 174–206.

Hernandez, J. S. (1991). Assisted performance in reading comprehension strategies with non-English proficient students. *The Journal of Educational Issues of Language Minority Students, 8,* 91–112.

Jacob, E., L. Rottenberg, S. Patrick, & E. Wheeler. (1996). Cooperative learning: Context and opportunities for acquiring academic English. *TESOL Quarterly, 30,* 253–280.

Johnson, D. W., & R. T. Johnson. (1989). Cooperative learning: What special educators need to know. *The Pointer, 33,* 5–10.

Kagan, S. (1986). Cooperative learning and sociocultural factors in schooling. In California State Department of Education, *Beyond language: Social and cultural factors in schooling language minority students* (pp. 231–298). Los Angeles: California State University, Evaluation, Dissemination and Assessment Center.

Kim, A. (2000, October). *The effect sizes for Collaborative Strategic Reading.* Paper presented at the Annual Meeting of the Council for Learning Disabilities, Austin, TX.

Klingner, J. K., & S. Vaughn. (1996). Reciprocal teaching of reading comprehension strategies for students with learning disabilities who use English as a second language. *Elementary School Journal, 96,* 275–293.

Klingner, J. K., & S. Vaughn. (1999). Promoting reading comprehension, content learning, and English acquisition through collaborative strategic reading (CSR). *The Reading Teacher, 52,* 738–747.

Klingner, J. K., S. Vaughn, & J. S. Schumm. (1998). Collaborative strategic reading during social studies in heterogeneous fourth-grade classrooms. *Elementary School Journal, 99,* 3–21.

Klingner, J. K., & S. Vaughn. (2000). The helping behaviors of fifth-graders while using collaborative strategic reading (CSR) during ESL content classes. *TESOL Quarterly, 34,* 69–98.

Klingner, J. K., M. T. Hughes, M. E. Arguelles, S. Ahwee, & S. Vaughn. (2001). *Outcomes for students with and without learning disabilities through Collaborative Strategic Reading.* Manuscript in progress.

Klingner, J. K., S. Vaughn, M. T. Hughes, J. S. Schumm, & B. Elbaum. (1998). Academic outcomes for students with and without learning disabilities in inclusive classrooms. *Learning Disabilities Research & Practice, 13,* 153–160.

Long, M., & P. Porter. (1985). Group work, interlanguage talk, and second language acquisition. *TESOL Quarterly, 19,* 207–228.

Madden, N. A., & R. E. Slavin. (1983). Mainstreaming students with mild handicaps: Academic and social outcomes. *Review of Educational Research, 53,* 519–569.

Palincsar, A. S., & A. L. Brown. (1984). The reciprocal teaching of comprehension-fostering and comprehension-monitoring activities. *Cognition and Instruction, 1,* 117–175.

Pressley, M., R. Brown, P. B. El-Dinary, & P. Afflerbach. (1995). The comprehension instruction that students need: Instruction fostering constructively responsive reading. *Learning Disabilities Research and Practice, 10,* 215–224.

Richard-Amato, P. A. (1992). Peer teachers: The neglected resource. In P. A. Richard-Amato & M. A. Snow (Eds.), *The multicultural classroom: Readings for content-area teachers* (pp. 271–284). White Plains, NY: Longman.

Rosenshine, B., & C. Meister. (1992). The use of scaffolds for teaching higher-level cognitive strategies. *Educational Leadership, 49,* 26–33.

Stevens, R. J., & R. E. Slavin. (1995). Effects of a cooperative learning approach in reading and writing on academically handicapped and nonhandicapped students. *The Elementary School Journal, 95,* 241–262.

Vaughn, S., D. Chard, D. P. Bryant, M. Coleman, B. Tyler, S. L. Thompson & K. Kouzekanani. (2000). Fluency and comprehension interventions for third-grade students: Two paths to improved fluency. *Remedial and Special Education, 21*(6), 325–335.

Weisberg, R. (1988). 1980's: A change in focus of reading comprehension research: A review of reading/learning disabilities research based on an interactive model of reading. *Learning Disability Quarterly, 11,* 149–159.

In this chapter we provide an overview and lesson plans for teaching CSR comprehension strategies to your students. These strategies teach students the metacognitive and self-regulation skills they need to comprehend well. To assist you in accomplishing this goal, the comprehension strategies are presented using the properties of explicit reading comprehension instruction, scaffolded instruction, and through

Teaching the CSR Comprehension Strategies to Your Class

demonstrations and think-alouds. Let's go through these seemingly esoteric terms so you will understand the rationale behind the design of the lessons you are about to teach.

Metacognition

Metacognition is the awareness and regulation of one's thinking processes, that is, thinking about your thinking. Metacognition is made up of two components: *metacognitive knowledge* (awareness) and *self-regulation knowledge* (regulation).

Chapter at a Glance

- **Introduction to the Lesson Plans**
  1. Metacognition
  2. Explicit Reading Comprehension Instruction
  3. Teaching Metacognition
  4. Lesson Plan Format

- **The CSR Lesson Plans**
  1. Overview of the Strategic Reading Process
  2. Preview
  3. Click and Clunk
  4. Get the Gist
  5. Wrap Up (Questioning)
  6. Wrap Up (Review)
  7. Putting It All Together

* **Metacognitive Knowledge** is the ability to know and use the strategies needed to successfully comprehend what is being read. Cognitive scientists have identified three categories of metacognitive knowledge: declarative, procedural, and conditional knowledge.

  * *Declarative Knowledge* is stored in memory in the form of facts, rules, concepts, strategies, etc. Examples of declarative knowledge are students' knowledge and understanding of the rules of grammar and punctuation or the steps of a reading comprehension strategy.

  * *Procedural Knowledge* refers to the way one's declarative knowledge (facts, rules, concepts, strategies, etc.) is executed. Students use procedural knowledge when they demonstrate a skill or a strategy. For example, students who can say the steps of the strategy for generating main idea statements possess declarative knowledge. Students who can *perform* the steps of the strategy automatically demonstrate procedural knowledge.

  * *Conditional Knowledge* is knowing when and under what conditions a strategy should be used. For example, when good readers' comprehension is interrupted by an encounter with an unknown word, they tap their conditional knowledge when they choose the appropriate strategy to resolve the problem.

* **Self-Regulation** involves monitoring, evaluating, and self-correcting activities. Self-regulation refers to the readers' ability to continually monitor and evaluate their comprehension and to implement strategies when comprehension breaks down. Evaluating involves self-checking activities that enable the reader to continually assess how comprehension is proceeding. Regulating activities are the strategies readers use to remediate difficulties in comprehension.

Explicit Reading Comprehension Instruction

Scaffolded Instruction

Explicit reading comprehension instruction is a vehicle to teach students the metacognitive knowledge and self-regulation skills they need to understand what they read. It is based on Vygotsky's work (1978) using scaffolded instruction and thinking aloud. Scaffolding is a process that enables students to solve a problem or achieve a goal that they could not accomplish on their own. The teacher works on strategies that are emerging in the students' repertoire but are underdeveloped. Vygotsky believed that these emerging skills were in the student's zone of proximal development. His research demonstrated that, with support, students could master those emerging skills. Vygotsky referred to that instructional support as scaffolded instruction.

The lessons we developed to teach the reading comprehension strategies in this book are based on the three phases of scaffolded instruction: modeling, teacher assistance, and independent. The teacher first models the thinking process by actually thinking aloud for the students. That is, the teacher demonstrates each facet of a strategy by explaining, in a step-by-step fashion, the thought processes used to draw a conclusion, make an inference, or generate a main idea statement.

During the teacher assisted phase, the teacher becomes more of a facilitator or coach as students become more automatic in implementing the strategy. In this phase, you are going to be asking more questions and providing guidance rather than modeling. When students reach the independent phase, they can complete the strategy automatically with minimal guidance from the teacher.

For example, in the CSR Lesson Plans, Lesson 2: Preview—Modeling Phase has the teacher thinking aloud and modeling the brainstorming and predicting procedures of the Preview strategy. As students become more facile with the process, the teacher moves to Lesson 3:

Preview—Teacher Assisted Phase, where students are guided through the process of thinking about what they know about a topic and predicting what they think they will learn and then writing these statements in their Learning Log. Lesson 4: Preview—Independent Phase is taught when students' proficiency indicates that they are ready to implement the strategy without assistance from the teacher. When students can Preview independently, they proceed to Lesson 5: Click and Clunk—Modeling Phase. The recursive procedure of scaffolded instruction is used to teach all four of the reading comprehension strategies.

Using scaffolded instruction to teach CSR is efficient because it allows you to use content area textbooks as a means to teach the comprehension strategies. In other words, you teach the subject matter and the comprehension strategies simultaneously. The lessons are designed so that, after teaching the strategy using a portion of the day's reading material, you can teach the remainder the way you would normally. For example, if your students are ready for Lesson 5: Click and Clunk—Modeling Phase, they would independently Preview the reading material you want to teach during the lesson; then, you would use a portion of that reading material to model the Click and Clunk strategy. After the strategy has been modeled, you can teach the remaining content using oral or silent reading, followed by class discussions, comprehension questions, or other activities of your choice.

Teaching Metacognition

We have infused metacognitive instruction into explicit strategy instruction by designing the Collaborative Strategic Reading lessons around four critical questions:

* What is the strategy?

* When is the strategy used?

* Why is it important to use this strategy?

* How is the strategy performed?

What is the strategy?

This question addresses students' Declarative Knowledge by explaining the components of the strategy. For example, during the Modeling Phase of the Preview strategy, students are taught that the strategy is composed of two parts: brainstorming what they know about a topic and predicting what they think they might learn.

When is the strategy used?

Conditional Knowledge is tapped when students can discuss when (or under what conditions) the strategy is used. During the Modeling Phase of the Preview strategy, students learn that they should brainstorm and predict *before* they start reading.

Why is it important to use this strategy?

When students understand why a strategy is important, we have tapped their Declarative and Conditional Knowledge. Declarative Knowledge is tapped when students are able to generally state why each strategy is important. This differs from Conditional Knowledge, where students are reading, experience a break down in comprehension, select a specific strategy based on the situation, and know why it is important for them to use it.

How is the strategy performed?

Procedural Knowledge is tapped when students can implement the strategy automatically and independently. Students demonstrate Procedural Knowledge of the Preview strategy when they can independently skim the reading assignment by looking at titles, subheading, graphs, or pictures, or if they locate key words and then generate brainstorming statements (what they already know about the topic) and predictions.

The Lesson Plan Format

There are 17 lessons in this manual. The first lesson provides an introduction to CSR and the last lesson combines all of the CSR strategies. The 15 lessons in between follow a recursive format based on the three phases of scaffolded instruction: the Modeling Phase, Teacher Assisted Phase, and Independent Phase. Each strategy is taught in three lessons. For example, after the introductory lesson, the next three lessons address the Preview strategy and consist of: Lesson 2: Preview—Modeling Phase, Lesson 3: Preview—Teacher Assisted Phase, and Lesson 4: Preview—Independent Phase. This same cycle is used to teach Click and Clunk, Get the Gist, and the two parts of Wrap Up: Questioning and Reviewing.

The lesson plans follow a consistent format. The teacher and student materials are listed first, followed by the objective of the lesson and teaching procedures. Script-like lessons are found in the Modeling Phase of each strategy. We feel that the lessons in the Modeling Phase should provide a crystal-clear illustration of how to accomplish this task. Since the purpose of this type of wording is to guide your instruction, we suggest that you read the lesson to get a clear picture of its content but teach the lesson using your own words and unique style! Italics indicate examples of what you might say to your students.

At the end of every Modeling Phase lesson, you see a box containing a sample *think-aloud* for the strategy being addressed. It can be difficult to explain thinking aloud. Therefore, we thought it would be helpful to provide a specific example of a think-aloud for each strategy. The reading material for the think-aloud samples is on the next page. Before teaching each lesson, be sure to reread the material so you can see how the think-aloud was generated based on the text. These examples will help you model the thinking processes for the reading material you use to teach CSR.

Although we call these "lessons," we do not want to convey that you must teach one lesson a day in a strict format. You should use the lessons flexibly, based on the needs of your students. Some students may take longer to learn the strategies and require additional lessons, whereas other students may need less time and can proceed through these lessons quickly, perhaps covering more than one in a day. Also, over the years we have each developed our own style of teaching CSR. Each of us teaches it a little differently, and we believe that you should feel free to adjust the instruction to fit your style and preferences.

Seabirds

A seabird is any bird that spends most of its time at sea and depends on the sea and its islands for all its basic needs. The see provides food, and its remote islands and rocky outcroppings provide safe nesting and resting places. For 60 million years, these highly specialized and diverse birds have adapted to life on the world's vast oceans.

Most of the 8,600 species of birds worldwide spend their lives in the air and on land. Only 260 or so of those species live in the air and on the sea. The differing habitats of deserts, mountains, and tropics are obvious for birds that are at home on land. But the sea is subtle. It may look like endless, unchanging ocean, but it offers a variety of habitats. Seabirds live in polar waters, equatorial waters, areas of cold water currents, upwellings, and other places where the water is turbulent and they find the most food. Fish feed in these areas because the turbulence, or motion of water, stirs the nutritive brew that promotes a rich growth of plankton. Fish feed on plankton, and seabirds eat a lot of fish.

Seabirds share a life at sea, but they have adapted to it in widely different ways. Some fly for months at a time, others can't fly at all. Some come ashore only to nest, others come ashore each night to roost. Most have waterproof plumage, some do not. None walk well because they are not adapted to life on land.

One particularly skilled seabird can't even swim! The frigatebird can only fly and perch, but it's acrobatics in the air win it all the food it wants. It is an aerial pirate, chasing, attacking, and stealing food from other birds. It gets its name from the frigates or man-o'-war ships sailed by pirates.

Life at sea seems healthy for the specially adapted seabirds. They have far longer lifespans than most birds. Depending on the species, seabirds can live to be 30, 40, or 50 years old. Only since people began to invade their remote islands and introduce predators have some seabirds become endangered.

Source: Wildlife Education, Ltd., ZOOBOOKS 12(7), April 1996. 9820 Willow Creek Road, Suite 300, San Diego, CA 92131.

Introduction: Overview of the Strategic Reading Process

We think that Collaborative Strategic Reading is best introduced by demonstrating the entire CSR process, either with a video or modeled by a group of students who already know CSR. This provides students with a picture of what they will be asked to do. The students who do not know CSR should not be expected to learn everything they see from the experienced group, but it will give them an overview of where they are going.

Teacher Materials

* CSR Video or a Group of Students Proficient in CSR

* Overhead Projector

* CSR's Plan for Strategic Reading Transparency Master (available at the end of Chapter 4)

Student Materials

* Nothing (or you may wish to provide students with a copy of the reading passage used by the group of students in the demonstration)

Lesson Objective

* To provide students with an overview of CSR by demonstrating the four strategies: Preview, Click and Clunk, Get the Gist, and Wrap Up.

Teaching Procedures

Explain to the class that you will be teaching them Collaborative Strategic Reading or "CSR." Define the terms: Collaborative (to work together), Strategic Reading (a plan or strategy to help them understand and remember what they read). CSR has four strategies that will help them understand and remember what they read. These strategies are what good readers do when they read, often automatically and "in their heads." Show students the CSR Plan for Strategic Reading. Tell students that you are going to show them how CSR works by demonstrating all four strategies. Show the video or ask your volunteer group of students to use the CSR strategies while reading a brief passage. Allow time for students to ask questions or share their impressions afterwards.

Lesson 2

Preview: Modeling Phase

The Preview strategy can be taught during social studies, science, or language arts. We often teach it using a short passage from *Weekly Reader* or another source for expository text. It is helpful if the story has a few headings and at least one illustration.

Teacher Materials

* Overhead projector
* Overhead: Preview strategy
* Overhead: Learning Log

Student Materials

* A copy of the reading passage for each student

Lesson Objective

* To model the brainstorm and prediction strategies students need to access background knowledge and set a purpose for reading.

Teaching Procedures

Sample Introduction to Preview

Ask something such as: *How many of you have ever been to the movies? I would like you to raise your hand if you have ever been to the movies to see a show. Good, it looks like most of you have done that. Now, when you go to the movies, and you get there on time, you often get a chance to see a very, very short movie about future shows that will be coming. What do we call these? That's right, we call these "Previews". How many of you like to see Previews? Yes, sometimes the Previews are the best part of going to the movies. OK, when you see a Preview about a movie, what do you learn?*

Call on students and prompt and nudge them until they identify the following:

* You learn about the setting
* You learn about the characters
* You learn about when the story takes place
* You learn about the key ideas in the story
* You learn about the stories genre or the type of story it will be
* You get a sense for whether or not you will like the story

Write these ideas on the chalkboard or on the overhead projector.

Say something like: *All right, so you can learn a great deal about a movie when you see a Preview—even though the Preview doesn't last very long.*

What is the strategy?

The first CSR strategy is called Preview. Previewing has two parts:

1. Brainstorming what you know about the topic.

2. Predicting what you think you will learn about the topic.

When is the strategy used?

Preview before you start reading the assigned material.

Why is it important to use the strategy?

Thinking about what you already know and predicting what you will learn helps you understand what you read and makes you more interested in what you will be reading.

How is the strategy performed?

When you Preview, look at the title, subheadings, pictures, captions, and graphs, etc., and skim the text to look for key words. Many times the key words are in dark or bold print. Model this concept for students.

Next you "brainstorm." That means you think of everything you already know about the topic. It could be something that you read, saw in a movie or on TV, or heard friends talk about. Think aloud for students by telling them what you already know about the day's topic. Write your ideas on the Learning Log transparency and tell students why you put each item on your list.

Sample Think-Aloud: Brainstorm

When I brainstorm, I think about what I already know about the topic, Seabirds. It could be something that I read, saw in a movie, on TV or heard friends talk about. I don't know very much about seabirds, but I will list what I know in my Learning Log.

---

* *Seabirds live around water.*

* *I can see from the picture that there are different types of seabirds.*

* *I can also see that seabirds dive into the water to get fish to eat.*

Then you predict. Predict means to take a guess at what you might learn. I am going to list my predictions for you. List your predictions. Think aloud by telling the students what information you used to come up with the prediction (e.g., titles, pictures, etc.). Write your ideas on the CSR Learning Log transparency.

Sample Think-Aloud: Predict

When I Predict I take a guess at what might happen or what I might learn. I will list what I predict I will learn in my Learning Log.

* *I see different types of birds so I predict that I will learn the names of some seabirds.*

* *If there are different types of birds, I predict I will learn what different types of food they eat.*

* *I see numbers in the passage. I predict I will learn how many types of birds there are and how long they live.*

* *I predict I will learn where they build their nests.*

Teach the remainder of the reading selection the way you normally would (round robin reading, silent reading, answering questions, class discussions, etc.). At the end of the lesson, discuss your brainstorming ideas and predictions by confirming or revising them.

Preview: Teacher Assisted Phase

Teacher Materials

* Overhead projector
* Overhead: Learning Log

Student Materials

* A copy of the reading passage for each student
* A Learning Log for each student (templates available in the Materials section of Chapter 4)

Lesson Objectives

* Students will answer questions about the Preview strategy.
* Students will be guided through the Preview strategy to determine what they think they know about a topic and to predict what they think they will learn.

Teaching Procedures

Reviewing Preview

Ask students what they remember about the Preview strategy. The following questions will help.

* *What does Preview mean?* (Look over what you are going to read so that you get an idea of what it will be about.)
* *When is the Preview strategy used?* (Before reading.)
* *Why is it important to use this strategy?* (Previewing helps you use what you already know and what you think you will learn to help you understand what you read.)
* *What are the two parts of the Preview strategy?* (Brainstorm and predict.)
* *What do you do first?* (Skim information in the text, such as the title, subheadings, pictures, graphs, and key words.)
* *What do you do during brainstorming?* (Think of everything you already know about the topic.)
* *Where could you have learned about the topic?* (Reading, movies, TV, friends, the internet, etc.)
* *What does predict mean?* (To take a guess at what you might learn.)
* *Where do you write your brainstorming ideas and predictions?* (In the Learning Log.)

Show students where to write their brainstorming ideas and predictions using the Learning Log transparency.

Previewing With Teacher Assistance

* Introduce the day's topic.
* Skim the text with the students.
* Ask students to brainstorm or think about what they saw while skimming the text and be ready to tell at least one thing they know or think they know about the topic.
* Call on students.

* Record students' brainstorming ideas in the Brainstorm section of the Learning Log.

* After a few students have shared, ask the class to write what they know in their Learning Logs.

* Ask students to think about what they saw while skimming the text and be ready to tell at least one thing they predict they might learn.

* Call on students. When a student has a particularly good prediction, ask him or her to explain to the rest of the class how he or she came up with that prediction.

* Record students' predictions in the Predict section of the Learning Log.

* After a few students have shared, ask the class to write what they might learn in their Learning Logs.

If students seem to be uncertain how to apply the Preview strategies, or do so in only cursory ways, "think aloud" how you would Preview the passage. Talk aloud to the class about the critical ideas, the heading, what you already know about the topic, and what you think it might be about.

Teach the remainder of the reading selection the way you normally would (round robin reading, silent reading, answering questions, class discussions, etc.). At the end of the lesson, have students confirm or revise their brainstorming ideas and predictions. Repeat this lesson with different reading material until students are ready to begin the Independent Phase of Preview.

Preview: Independent Phase

Teacher Materials

* Overhead projector
* Overhead: Learning Log

Student Materials

* A copy of a reading passage for each student
* A Learning Log for each student

Lesson Objective

* Students will work with a partner to skim the text and write what they know and what they might learn about the topic.

Teaching Procedures

Previewing Independently

Tell students that you are going to ask them to work with partners today to construct a preview of what they are about to read. First review the procedures that they will use for Previewing. Through questioning and revising what students suggest for a Preview, help them to recall the following Preview steps.

* Look at the title
* Look at the first and last sentence

* Look at the pictures or illustrations
* Read the headings
* Read the words that are bold or in italics
* Think of what you already know about this topic
* Predict what you think it will be about

Brainstorm

* Ask students to brainstorm and write what they think they know about the topic in their Learning Logs.
* Tell them how many minutes they will have to complete the task and set the timer.
* Circulate among students while they are working to provide assistance as needed
* After the timer sounds, allow several pairs an opportunity to read aloud what they have brainstormed. Provide feedback to students.

Predict

* Ask students to think about what they saw while skimming the selection and write what they predict they might learn in their Learning Logs.
* Tell them how many minutes they will have to complete the task and set the timer.
* Circulate among students while they are working to provide assistance as needed.
* After the timer sounds, allow several pairs an opportunity to read their predictions aloud. Ask other students to provide feedback about how effective they think these predictions are. Provide feedback to students.

Teach the remainder of the reading selection the way you normally would (round robin reading, silent reading, answering questions, class discussions, etc.). At the end of the lesson, have students confirm or revise their predictions. Repeat this lesson with different reading material until students are ready to begin the Modeling Phase of Click and Clunk.

We suggest that you continue to practice Previews across content areas and during reading instruction. Most students already have had adequate opportunities to identify and write Previews and they acquire this strategy relatively quickly. For students who need additional time or practice, it is highly appropriate to wait until they are better able to conduct Previews with minimal support from the teacher, but in pairs, before moving to the next strategy.

Frequently Asked Questions About Preview

1. *Do students need to work in pairs after I initially model and explain how to do a Preview?*

   It is up to the teacher whether students work alone or in pairs. We think that there are advantages to giving students opportunities to learn to work together on constructing Previews. Some teachers have students work in small groups, but our experience is that when students are **first** introduced to the strategy, they have more opportunities to practice it if they work alone or with one other student.

2. *When students write their Previews does each student write one? What format do the Previews need to be in?*

   Remember the goal of previewing is to get students to scan the text, look for critical information, trigger their background knowledge, and prepare them to read. We do not want this exercise to take very long—no more than eight minutes total. For this reason, the Preview can be more like "notes" or "key ideas" rather than complete sentences.

3. *Isn't a Preview the same thing as KWL?[1]*

   The Preview strategy is very similar to KWL. Both strategies encourage students to search text to look for critical ideas and then to think about what they already know to link it to these critical ideas. One of the significant differences is that with CSR students learn to predict what they will learn about from reading the text.

4. *When might the teacher want to conduct a whole class Preview?*

   When the text that students are asked to read contains unfamiliar information or concepts, the teacher may want to conduct a whole class Preview to introduce students to the new ideas and vocabulary. Some teachers may also want to conduct whole class Previews when the text they are reading is familiar because it is linked to previous lessons. The teacher may want to assist students in linking what they already have learned to the new text.

---

[1] KWL (Ogle, 1986) is a strategy for increasing students' engagement with expository text. The teacher or students prepare a K-W-L chart on the chalkboard, chart paper, an overhead transparency, or a sheet of paper. The chart is divided into three columns, the first with a K at the top, the second with a W, and the third with an L. Before reading, the teacher and students brainstorm what they already Know about the topic they will be studying and record this information in the K column of the chart. Next, still before reading, students generate questions about What they would like to learn about the topic and write these questions in the second column. Finally, after reading, students record what they Learned as a result of the day's lesson in the third column of their charts.

Click and Clunk: Modeling Phase

There are many ways and times to introduce the next strategy, Click and Clunk. Click and Clunk prompts students to focus on their understanding of whatever text they are reading, across the curriculum, and provides them with steps they can follow to fix their comprehension whenever it breaks down. Thus it can be introduced during language arts as well as during content area instruction. You may already have taught your students what to do when they encounter words they don't know. We've found it very useful for teachers and students alike to be able to attach the "Click and Clunk" vocabulary to these challenging words.

When teaching the Click and Clunk strategy to the whole class it is important to remember that the purpose is to teach students to monitor what they are reading and to think about concepts or words in the text that are causing them difficulty. Remember that we want students to think about what they are reading and to stop and reflect on what they don't understand, even if this means that students will need to write down a challenging word and learn more about it later.

Teacher Materials

- ✳ Overhead projector
- ✳ Overhead: Click and Clunk
- ✳ Overhead: Learning Log

Student Materials

- ✳ A copy of the reading passage for each student
- ✳ A Learning Log for each student

Lesson Objective

- ✳ To model using the fix-up strategies students need to determine the meaning of vocabulary they do not understand.

Teaching Procedures

Sample Introduction to Click and Clunk

The strategy you will learn today is called Click and Clunk. It will help you figure out words you do not understand. When you understand everything you are reading, everything "clicks" along smoothly. It's like driving your car without any speed bumps or roadblocks in the way. When you do not understand a word, "clunk," you stop, sort of like running into a brick wall or hitting a roadblock while driving. You really don't understand the point the author is making or a word that the author is using. Perhaps it is a new vocabulary word that is central to understanding the piece. That's a clunk. Proper nouns are not clunks because they usually do not affect the meaning of the story. Remember, hard words are clunks only if they keep you from understanding what you are reading.

What is the strategy?

Click and Clunk is when you think about what you are reading and check to make sure you understand everything. When you find words you don't understand, you figure out what they mean. We say that words or ideas we understand "click." Words or ideas we don't understand "clunk."

When is the strategy used?

You are going to use the strategy while you are reading, stopping after each paragraph or section of text to figure out your clunks.

Why is it important to use this strategy?

It is important to identify clunks and to figure them out to help you understand what you are reading.

How is the strategy performed?

I am going to show you how to use the strategy. I will read the first paragraph. As I read, I am going to make a mental note of the words I do not understand. (Read the first paragraph.) *I had trouble understanding the word _____. That is a clunk. There are four fix-up strategies to help figure out clunks.* (Use the Clunk Fix-Up Strategies transparency.)

Reread the sentence with the clunk and look for key ideas to help you figure out the word. Think about what makes sense.

Reread the sentences before and after the clunk, looking for clues.

Look for a prefix or suffix in the word that might help.

Break the word apart and look for smaller words that you know.

I will start with the first fix-up strategy. I will reread the sentence with the clunk and look for key ideas to help me figure out the word. (Go through the fix-up strategies until you find the one that helps you figure out the meaning of the word. Remember to think aloud so students will learn how you figured out the meaning of the word. Write the definition on the Learning Log transparency.)

> **Sample Think-Aloud: Click and Clunk**
>
> *I don't know what "remote" means. That's a clunk. I'll read the sentence again and look for clues that help me understand. The sentence says, "The sea provides food, and its remote islands and rocky outcroppings provide safe nesting and resting places." If the remote islands are safe places for nesting and resting, then that could mean that remote means the islands are far away from anything that could hurt them. So, in my Learning Log I am going to write that remote means far away.*

With subsequent paragraphs, ask students to identify clunks. Say something like: *OK, now I'm going to read to you the next paragraph and I want you to listen carefully and decide if any words or ideas are clunks for you. As I read and you hear a "clunk" I want you to write it down and we will discuss the clunks as a class when I am finished reading.*

After reading another paragraph, ask students to raise their hands if they have any clunks. Clunks that are identified by several students or that you think are essential to understanding the text should be taught to students. Model usage of the "fix-up" strategies using a "think-aloud" procedure.

Repeat this process with the next paragraph in the passage. Ask students who do not raise their hands whether they understand all of the words and concepts that you have just read. If yes, identify a few difficult words or concepts. Then model how to figure out the meaning of these words, again using a "think-aloud" procedure. Next, ask students to explain what the words mean. It is important that students learn to listen or read carefully to make sure that they detect words or concepts they do not understand.

Teach the remainder of the reading selection the way you normally would (round robin reading, silent reading, answering questions, class discussions, etc.). In subsequent lessons and throughout each day, encourage students to detect words, ideas, or concepts that they don't understand. Some teachers refer to their students as "clunk detectors" and praise students who are effective at finding "clunks" and unpacking them.

Lesson 6

Click and Clunk: Teacher Assisted Phase

After students learn to recognize clunks, they also need to learn to implement the strategies that assist them in "declunking" difficult words and ideas. Fix-up strategies assist students in repairing the meaning of challenging text.

Teacher Materials

* Overhead projector
* Overhead: Learning Log
* Overhead: Click and Clunk

Student Materials

* A copy of the reading passage for each student
* Learning Log for each student

Lesson Objective

* Students answer questions about the Click and Clunk strategy, identify vocabulary they do not understand, and are guided through the fix-up strategies to determine the meaning of the vocabulary.

Teaching Procedures

Reviewing the Click and Clunk Strategy

Ask students what they remember about the Click and Clunk strategy. The following questions will help.

* *What does it mean when you are clicking while you are reading?* (You understand everything.)

* *What does it mean when you clunk while you are reading?* (You do not understand something.)

* *Are proper nouns clunks?* (No.)

* *Why?* (Because they usually do not affect the meaning of the story.)

* *Are hard words always clunks?* (No, only if they keep you from understanding what you are reading.)

* *When do you use this strategy?* (While you are reading.)

* *Why is it important to identify clunks and figure them out?* (It helps you understand what you read.)

* *How do we figure out clunks?* (You use the four fix-up strategies.)

* *What are the four fix-up strategies?*

  1. Reread the sentence with the clunk and look for key ideas to help you figure out the word. Think about what makes sense.

  2. Reread the sentences before and after the clunk, looking for clues.

  3. Look for a prefix or suffix in the word that might help.

  4. Break the word apart and look for smaller words that you know.

Click and Clunk With Teacher Assistance

✳ Read the first paragraph (or section) of the passage aloud (or ask students to do this).

✳ Remind students to make a mental note of the words they do not understand.

✳ Ask students to write their clunks in their Learning Log. Use the Learning Log transparency to show students where to write their clunks.

✳ Ask who would like to share a clunk.

✳ Tell the class to locate the clunk in the passage and write it in their Learning Log if they haven't already done so.

✳ Ask the student to state the first fix-up strategy. Use Clunk Fix-Up Strategies transparency.

✳ Apply the fix-up strategy: Ask all students to go back to the paragraph and reread the sentence with the clunk in it, thinking about what would make sense.

✳ Ask the students if that fix-up strategy helped. If that helped students to figure out the clunk, make sure to ask them to explain how they came up with the meaning.

✳ If that fix-up strategy did not help, go to the next one and follow the same procedure. After the clunk is figured out, have all students write the definition in their Learning Logs. Use the Learning Log transparency to show students where to write their definition in the Learning Log.

✳ Read the next paragraph using the same procedure. Continue the procedure of reading and figuring out clunks for several paragraphs.

Teach the remainder of the reading selection the way you normally would (e.g., answering questions, class discussions). Repeat this lesson with different reading material until students are ready to begin the Independent Phase of Click and Clunk.

Many students benefit from additional practice in learning to apply fix-up strategies. You might wish to do this using the practice sentences provided in the Materials section at the end of Chapter 4. Each sentence or cluster of sentences has a different clunk that can be "declunked" with one or more of the fix-up strategies (e.g., "Everyday Michele runs, rides her bike, and swims. She hopes that some day she can be a triathlete in the Olympics." "Anthony's favorite pastime is listening to his parents' old jazz records." "The United States exports more goods to China now that the two countries have reached a trade agreement."). We suggest that you copy these onto overhead transparencies and present them to students one at a time. Direct students to work with their partners to figure out the meaning of the underlined word *and* to decide which of the fix-up strategies is most helpful.

Lesson 7

Click and Clunk: Independent Phase

Teacher Materials

* Overhead projector
* Overhead: Learning Log

Student Materials

* A copy of the reading passage for each student
* A Learning Log for each student

Lesson Objective

* Students will independently use the fix-up strategies to determine the meaning of vocabulary they do not understand.

Teaching Procedures

* Have students work in pairs.
* Read the first paragraph (or section) of the passage aloud (or ask students to do this).
* Tell students how many minutes they will have to:
    * Find clunks and write them in their Learning Logs.

* Use the fix-up strategies to figure out what the clunks mean. (Show the Clunk Fix-up Strategies transparency.)
* Write the meanings of the clunks in their Learning Logs.
* Set the timer.
* While students are working, circulate among them and help with "declunking" as necessary. Note which clunks are the most troublesome for students.
* After the timer sounds, **either** continue with the next paragraph using the same procedure or review with students how they figured out a clunk that was particularly troublesome, and then continue with the next paragraph. Continue this for the remainder of the passage.

At the end of the lesson, elicit students' clunks and their definitions. Ask a few students to write their clunks and definitions on an overhead transparency so that all of the students can see them, and then ask other students if they agree with the definitions, or perhaps have a different version. Students who come up with a really good definition should be asked to explain how they figured out the clunk. Finish the lesson the way you normally would (e.g., with a class discussion, answering questions). Repeat this lesson with different reading material until students are ready to begin Lesson 8, the Modeling Phase of Get the Gist.

Frequently Asked Questions About Click and Clunk

1. *What role does the dictionary play in helping students understand "clunks"?*

   While learning to use the dictionary is an important part of vocabulary and reading development, we suggest that students *not* use dictionaries during CSR as a fix-up strategy. The goal of Click and Clunk is for students to learn to figure out words on their own from clues they find in the text and by using their own background knowledge. After all, students aren't allowed to use dictionaries while taking high stakes tests. However, checking definitions in a dictionary *after* CSR can be an effective follow-up activity.

2. *I have students who are almost non-readers and they can't even read the words. How can they do Click and Clunk?*

We have seen CSR implemented quite effectively in inclusion classrooms that include nonreaders. Peers help each other identify words, quickly and matter-of-factly. A word is only a clunk if its meaning is not *understood* once it has been identified—it's not just a word a student doesn't know how to read. CSR provides a format where students can participate, learn content material, and improve their reading.

3. *I have students who are English language learners. Won't they have too much difficulty with this?*

CSR has been used successfully in linguistically diverse classrooms with students ranging in proficiency from beginning levels upward. The cooperative group structure provides an environment where students help each other learn. Bilingual peers can be quite good at determining when an unknown word simply needs a quick translation because the concept is understood in the student's native language, or when a more elaborate explanation is needed (see Klingner & Vaughn, 2000).

Get the Gist: Modeling Phase

When students are relatively proficient at Click and Clunk it is appropriate to teach the next strategy to the whole class, Get the Gist. The central idea behind Get the Gist is to teach students how to find the main idea of a passage.

Teacher Materials

* Overhead projector
* Overhead: Learning Log
* Overhead: Get the Gist
* Blank overhead

Student Materials

* A copy of the reading passage for each student
* Learning Log for each student

Lesson Objective

* To model the steps for generating main idea statements.

Teaching Procedures

Sample Introduction to Get the Gist

Today I am going to demonstrate the next CSR strategy, Get the Gist. When you Get the Gist, you think about the most important idea in the paragraph or section of text you have just finished reading. The gist is often called the main idea.

What is the strategy?
Get the Gist helps you figure out the most important ideas in what you just read. First, you think about the "who" or "what" the paragraph was mostly about, and then you figure out the most important ideas about the who or what and say this in ten words or less.

When is the strategy used?
You figure out the gist after reading each paragraph or section of text.

Why is it important to use this strategy?
Getting the gist is important because it helps you check whether you understand what you just finished reading. It also helps you remember what you read.

How is the strategy performed?
There are three steps to Getting the Gist of a paragraph (use the Get the Gist transparency):

* *First, name the who or what that the paragraph is mostly about.*
* *Second, tell the most important information about the who or what.*
* *Third, write a gist of ten words or less, leaving out details.*

Use the Learning Log transparency to show students where to write the gist.

Read a paragraph with your students and then say: *I am going to show you how to Get the Gist for the paragraph we just read. First, I figure out if the paragraph is about a "who" (a person) or a "what" (a place or thing). Then I will name the who or what the paragraph was mostly about. We call this the topic.* Tell the students the who or what the paragraph you just read is mostly about. Explain how you determined that answer and write the answer on a blank transparency.

Second, I will list the most important information about the who or what. Tell the students the most important information about the who or what and write the answers on the transparency.

Third, I will write a gist of ten words or less, leaving out details. There are three important things I need to remember about the gist:

✻ *The gist must be a complete sentence.*

✻ *The main who or what only counts as one word. For example, if the main who or what is The United States Senate, it only counts as one word.*

✻ *A good gist contains information that will help you remember the important details in a paragraph.*

Write the gist on the transparency. Think aloud and explain how a good gist contains information that will help you remember the important details in a paragraph. That is, the gist prompts you to recall the important information that was listed during the second step of the strategy.

Read the next paragraph. Model how to Get the Gist for this paragraph. Continue this cycle for the remaining paragraphs.

Sample Think-Aloud: Get the Gist

- ***First****, I am going to name who or what that the paragraph was mostly about. That would be **Seabirds**.*

- ***Second****, I am going to name the most important information about the who or what: **I learned that Seabirds live, get food, rest and nest at the sea.***

- ***Third****, I will say the gist in ten words or less leaving out details: **Seabirds get everything they need from the sea.***

Teach the remainder of the reading selection the way you normally would (round robin reading, silent reading, answering questions, class discussions, etc.).

Get the Gist: Teacher Assisted Phase

Teacher Materials

* Overhead projector
* Overhead: Learning Log
* Overhead: Get the Gist
* Blank overhead

Student Materials

* A copy of the reading passage for each student
* Learning Log for each student

Lesson Objectives

* Students will answer questions about the Get the Gist strategy.
* Students will be guided through the process of identifying the most important who or what in paragraphs, determining the most important information about the who or what, and generating main idea statements.

Teaching Procedures

Reviewing Get the Gist

Ask students what they remember about the Get the Gist strategy. The following questions will help.

* *What do we do when we Get the Gist?* (We write about the most important idea in the paragraph or section of text.)
* *When do we Get the Gist?* (After reading each paragraph or section of text.)
* *Why is getting the gist important?* (It helps us check whether we understand what we read and helps us remember what we read.)
* *When we Get the Gist, what do we leave out?* (Details)
* *What are three important things to remember about the gist?* (The gist must be a complete sentence. The main who or what only counts as one word. A good gist contains information that will help you remember the important details in a paragraph.)

Getting the Gist With Teacher Assistance

* Read the first paragraph (or section) in the day's passage (or ask students to do this).
* Ask students to tell you if the passage was mostly about a who (person) or a what (place or thing). Call on several students to determine if there is agreement about whether the passage was mostly about a "who" or a "what."
* After you have established whether the passage was about a "who" or "what," ask students to identify who or what it is about (the topic). Write the answer on the blank transparency.

* After students have determined the "topic" for the main idea statement, lead them in a class discussion to determine the most important information about the "topic." Be sure to emphasize that they are looking for the most essential information—not details. Write the answers on the transparency.

* Lead the students in writing a class gist of ten words or less. Select students to help you compose this main idea statement. If students contribute specific details, remind them that the main idea does not contain details; the main idea helps them remember the details in the paragraph. You may need to review main idea statements that you generated during the modeling phase to reinforce this concept. Consider writing more than one class gist for each paragraph. Write each gist on the transparency.

* Critique the gists by explaining how they either meet or do not meet the criterion that a good gist contains information that will help students remember the important details in a paragraph.

* As the students become proficient in writing class gists, have them write gists in pairs after you lead them in determining the "topic" and the most important information about the "topic."

Teach the remainder of the reading selection the way you normally would (round robin reading, silent reading, answering questions, class discussions, etc.). Repeat this lesson with different reading material until students are ready to begin the Independent Phase of Get the Gist.

Sample for the Teacher Assisted Phase of Get the Gist

Following is an illustration of how Mrs. Cally taught her fifth-grade students to Get the Gist. She began by giving students a short passage from the *Weekly Reader*. She asked them to read the first paragraph from the passage and while they were reading to think about what the story was mostly about. After they finished reading, she wrote the following words on the board: *person*, *place*, *thing*. Then she told students to identify whether the paragraph that they just read was mostly about a person, place, or a thing. All of the students agreed that it was mostly about a person. She then asked them to name the person it was mostly about, and the class agreed that it was Thomas Edison. She then asked them to tell her the most important points about Thomas Edison that appeared in the paragraph. As students responded, she asked other students whether they agreed. When there was consensus, she wrote them down in the form of notes on an overhead transparency. When they were finished, she asked students to look at the topic, Thomas Edison, and consider the key points and to work with their partner to write one sentence of ten words or less that tells the key information about Thomas Edison. Selected students then read their sentences aloud and Mrs. Cally asked students to assist her in determining whether the sentences were good gist sentences.

Get the Gist: Independent Phase

Teacher Materials

* Overhead projector
* Overhead: Learning Log

Student Materials

* A copy of the reading passage for each student
* Learning Log for each student

Lesson Objective

* Students will independently generate main idea statements by identifying the most important who or what in paragraphs and then determining the most important information about the who or what.

Teaching Procedures

Getting the Gist Independently

* Read a paragraph (or section of text) aloud (or have students do this).
* Ask students to work in pairs.
* Tell students how many minutes they will have to Get the Gist of the paragraph they just read and set the timer.

* While students are working, circulate among them and help them Get the Gist as necessary. Use the scaffolding techniques described earlier in this chapter.

* After the timer sounds, **either** have students proceed with the next paragraph (or section of text) **or** ask students to share their gist for a particularly challenging paragraph (and then proceed with the next paragraph). If most students seem to be able to Get the Gist proficiently for a specific paragraph, it is not necessary to stop the class at this point.

* Continue this cycle of reading a paragraph and having the students Get the Gist independently until the passage has been read.

After reading the entire day's selection:

* Call on a few students to share their gists with the class. Ask a few students to write their gists on an overhead transparency. As a class, discuss aspects of these gists that are strong and aspects that need improvement. Together write a class gist. The goal is to improve everyone's skills in writing gists.

Teachers can continue to practice Click and Clunk and Get the Gist across content areas and during reading instruction. Although most students generally acquire the Preview strategy relatively quickly, many students may need additional time or practice in figuring out clunks or writing gists. Remember that these skills can take considerable time to learn and to improve. Thus, continue to provide opportunities for students to explain how they figured out challenging words and to critique the gists of other students. Provide suggestions for how to make gists as strong as possible. After students have demonstrated some proficiency with the other strategies they are ready to learn to Wrap Up (Lesson 11).

Frequently Asked Questions About Get the Gist

1. *Is it OK if students' sentences are longer than ten words?*

   The purpose of making sentences ten words or less is to provide structure so that students only include the most essential information. Otherwise, students write gist statements that are too long and repeat everything that is in the original passage. However, if teachers would like to omit this rule, that is certainly OK. We have found that some teachers like to emphasize this requirement while others do not.

2. *What if students just repeat a sentence or string of words from the passage when they write the gist?*

   The purpose of writing a gist is for students to learn to put the key ideas into their own words. For some students, learning to do this involves a sequence of steps that includes learning to identify the critical information from the passage and then learning to put it into their own words. At first, the teacher may accept key words from the passage as the gist. Eventually, students need to move to the point where they can paraphrase what is said by the author and write it themselves.

3. *My students already know how to find the main idea when they read. If I teach them to "Get the Gist," won't that confuse them?*

   Many students already know one or more of the CSR strategies. It is important to point out to students that "getting the gist" is the same as "finding the main idea" and that there can be different ways to name the same procedure. Challenge them to think of other examples.

4. *Do students always need to write down the gist?*

   No, some teachers may not want students to always write their gists, believing that doing so takes too much time. However, it is important that students always generate gists and discuss them with their peers.

Wrap Up (Questioning): Modeling Phase

The purpose of Wrap Up is for students to identify the critical information and key ideas across a large section of text—an entire passage (multiple paragraphs) or chapter. Wrap Up has two parts, Questioning and Review. First, you will teach students how to generate questions. We teach students about Question-Answer Relationships (QAR) during this strategy (Raphael, 1982, 1984, 1986).

Teacher Materials

* Overhead projector
* Overhead: Learning Log
* Overhead: Wrap Up
* Overhead: Question Types
* Overhead: Sample Question Stems
* Blank overhead

Student Materials

* A copy of the reading passage for each student (use a multiple-paragraph section of text that you have already read as a class)
* Learning Log for each student

Lesson Objective

* To model the steps for generating teacher-like questions.

Teaching Procedures

Sample Introduction to Wrap Up (Questioning)

Today we are going to learn about Wrap Up. Pay close attention, because I am going to share with you my secrets for making up the questions I use on quizzes and tests. When I'm preparing a test, I really want to make sure I ask you about the most important information you need to know, so first I go back and look at the book and identify the most important ideas. Then I use these key ideas to generate questions. I start each question with one of the W words, or an H (i.e., Who, What, Where, When, Why, or How). I make sure to come up with different kinds of questions (because that is what good teachers do). (Put up the transparency with question types.) *I want you to remember a few important facts straight from the passage, and so I ask questions that have the answer right there. Guess what? We call these "right there" questions. And of course I want you to think about what you are learning—so I ask some questions that have an answer in the passage but require you to look in different places and put ideas together. We call these "think and search" questions. The hardest kind of question doesn't have an answer in the passage. You have to think about what the author has written and what you already know. We call these "author and you" questions. Sometimes I use question stems to help me come up with really good "million dollar" questions.*

What is the strategy?

During Wrap Up you think of questions, ask questions, answer questions, and write what you learned. When you think of questions, think about the most important ideas that you have read.

When is the strategy used?

Wrap Up after finishing the day's reading assignment.

Why is it important to use the strategy?

Wrap Up helps you remember what you read and helps you prepare for tests and class discussions. It shows whether or not you understand the most important information you have read.

How is the strategy performed?

When you Wrap Up, you go over the important information you have learned by:

* ✳ *First, thinking of questions and writing them in the Learning Log.*

* ✳ *Second, reviewing what you have learned and writing it in the Learning Log.*

Sample Think-Aloud: "Right There" Questions

Question: *What is a seabird?*

Think-aloud: *The answer is in the first sentence: "A seabird is any bird that spends most of its time at sea and depends on the sea and its islands for all basic needs." This is a* **Right There** *question because the words used to make up the question and the words used to answer the question are* **Right There** *in the same sentence.*

Sample Think-Aloud: "Think and Search" Questions

Question: *Why do seabirds find most of their food in turbulent water?*

Think-aloud: *The answer is that turbulence stirs up the nutrients or minerals that help plankton grow. The fish gather around to eat the plankton and the seabirds eat the fish! This is a* **Think and Search** *question because in order to answer that question, you have to read to put together the information from the last three sentences in the second paragraph.*

Sample Think-Aloud: "Author and You" Questions

Question: *What causes seabirds to have a longer lifespan than most birds?*

Think-aloud: *Seabirds live longer because they live in places that are far from people who might kill or sell them and where there are no natural predators to kill them. This is an* **Author and You** *question because in the last paragraph, particularly the last sentence, the author gave me information* **clues** *that helped me answer the question. The author said that since people started coming to the islands and introducing predators (animals that will kill and eat the birds), some birds have become endangered. I know that one reason seabirds have a longer lifespan is because they live in places where they are safe because not many people are around to sell or kill them and there are no natural predators to kill the seabirds. So they live longer.*

Wrap Up (Questioning): Teacher Assisted Phase

Teacher Materials

* Overhead projector
* Overhead: Learning Log
* Overhead: Wrap Up
* Blank overhead

Student Materials

* A copy of the reading passage for each student (use a multiple-paragraph section of text that you have already read as a class)
* Learning Log for each student

Lesson Objective

* To assist students in generating teacher-like questions as part of the Wrap Up strategy.

Teaching Procedures

Reviewing Wrap Up (Questioning)

Before generating questions, ask the students what they remember about Wrap Up and Questioning. The following questions will help.

* *What is the first thing you do when you Wrap Up?* (Think of questions and write them in the Learning Log.)

* *When you think of questions, what do you think about?* (Think about the most important ideas in what you have read.)

* *When you think of questions, who do you pretend to be?* (The teacher and think of questions that might be asked on a test.)

* *Why do you ask questions?* (To show whether or not you know what you have read.)

* *With which words do questions begin?* (How or one of the "W" words: who, what, when, where, why.)

* *What is a Right There question?* (The words used to make up the question and the words used to answer the question are Right There in the same sentence.)

* *What is a Think and Search question?* (The answer to the question is in the reading, but it is made up of information that comes from more than one sentence or paragraph. You have to put together information from different parts of the reading to find the answer.)

* *What is an Author and You question?* (The answer to an Author and You question is not in the reading. To answer an Author and You question, you have to think about what the author tells you and what you already know.)

Questioning With Teacher Assistance

* Use text (multiple paragraphs) that the students have recently read. If necessary, give students an opportunity to skim or reread sections of the text.

* Lead the class in generating questions. Write the questions on the Learning Log transparency. After each question is generated, call on a student to answer it, label the question type, and explain the reason

for the label. As students become proficient in generating questions, skip this step and proceed to the next step.

* Give the students a few minutes to write questions in their Learning Logs. Use the Learning Log transparency to show students where to write the questions.

* After questions are generated, call on students to ask one of their questions.

* After each question is asked, call on a student to answer it, label the question type, and explain the reason for the label.

* As an alternate strategy, you can have students discuss the answer with a partner before calling on a student to answer the question, label the question type, and explain the reason for the label.

Sample for Teacher Assisted Questioning

Ms. Royal tells students that she would like them to help her write the kinds of questions that a good teacher would ask about what they just read. She tells them that she would like them to come up with some "right there," some "think and search," and some "author and you" questions. She also provides them with question stems to assist them in coming up with "million dollar" questions. She writes these question stems on an overhead projector, on a large chart, or on the chalkboard.

* What do you think would happen if _____?

* How would you compare and contrast _____?

* How do you think _____ could have been prevented?

* How were _____ and _____ the same? Different?

* How would you interpret _____?

* Who could have made a difference in the ending? _____

* What would they have had to do? _____

* Where did this take place? _____ Are there other places it could have occurred? _____?

* What do you think is the most important event in the story? _____ Why? _____

She tells students that the above questions are just examples of the kinds of questions that could be asked and that over time they will learn to ask better and better questions. She tells each pair of students that she would like for them to generate two questions about what they just read. They should write the questions and the answers in their Learning Logs. She allows students about ten minutes to complete the activity. When they have finished, she calls on pairs of students to read their questions and asks other students to help determine if there are ways to improve them. After several pairs of students have had a chance to read their questions and discuss how to make them better, she gives students five minutes to rewrite or revise their questions. After the five minutes, she asks students to identify how they changed their questions and provides them with feedback about the quality of their questions. She specifies that students should write both the questions and the answers in their Learning Logs.

Repeat this lesson with different reading material until students are ready to begin the Independent Phase of Questioning.

Wrap Up (Questioning): Independent Phase

Teacher Materials

* Overhead projector
* Overhead: Learning Log
* Overhead: Wrap Up
* Blank overhead

Student Materials

* A copy of the reading passage for each student (use a multiple-paragraph section of text that you have already read as a class)
* Learning Log for each student

Lesson Objective

* Students will generate teacher-like questions as part of the Wrap Up strategy.

Teaching Procedures

Generating Questions Independently

* Tell students they will be working in pairs.
* Tell students how many minutes they will have to generate questions and write them in their Learning Logs; set the timer.
* While students are working, circulate among them and provide assistance as needed. Note who comes up with really good questions that you'll want asked during your whole class follow up.
* After the timer sounds, call on different students to ask their questions and call on other students to answer them. Students' responses should include answering the question, labeling the question type, and explaining why the label is appropriate.

Once students have had some practice generating and answering each other's questions, they are ready for Review, the very last step in CSR.

Wrap Up (Review): Modeling Phase

The Review strategy is probably the easiest of all the strategies for students to learn. Students take just a few minutes (two or three) to write down the most important ideas they learned from the day's reading assignment in their CSR Learning Logs. The teacher then calls on various students to quickly share their favorite idea, thus providing a review of the day's learning.

Teacher Materials

* Overhead projector
* Overhead: Learning Log

Student Materials

* A copy of the reading passage for each student
* Learning Log for each student

Lesson Objective

* To model how to review information from the reading passage.

Teaching Procedures

Sample Introduction to Wrap Up (Review)

Today you are going to learn the very last step in CSR. Do you remember the second part of Wrap Up? That's right, it's called "Review". During Review you think about the important information you learned from the day's reading. What did you learn that you didn't know before? What did you learn that you thought was really interesting? These are the ideas that you write in your Learning Log.

What is the strategy?
During Review, you write about the important things you have learned from what you read.

When is the strategy used?
Review after asking and answering questions.

Why is it important to use this strategy?
Reviewing will help you remember what you read and help you prepare for tests and class discussions.

How is the strategy performed?
Think about the important information you learned and write it in your Learning Log.

Modeling the Review Strategy
The important information for this reading, is _____. Write important information from the passage on the Learning Log transparency.

Seabirds spend most of their time at sea. They live in cold water and warm water. They eat a lot of fish. Some seabirds fly while others cannot. They have a longer lifespan than most birds but some are becoming endangered.

Repeat this lesson with different reading material until students are ready to begin the Teacher Assisted Phase of Review.

Lesson 15

Wrap Up (Review): Teacher Assisted Phase

Teacher Materials

* Overhead projector
* Overhead: Learning Log

Student Materials

* A copy of the reading passage for each student
* Learning Log for each student

Lesson Objective

* Students will be guided through the process of summarizing information from the reading passage.

Teaching Procedures

Reviewing Wrap Up (Review)

What do you do when you review? (When you review, you think about the important information you learned from what you read. Then, you write it in the Learning Log.)

Review With Teacher Assistance

* Lead the students in writing a class list of the important information they have learned. Write this on the Learning Log transparency. As students become proficient in reviewing, skip this step and proceed to the next step.

* Give the students a few minutes (two to three) to write important information they have learned from the reading.

* Select students to share what they learned.

* As an alternate strategy, you can have students turn to a partner and share the most important information they have learned.

Repeat this lesson with different reading material until students are ready to begin the Independent Phase of Review.

Wrap Up (Review): Independent Phase

Teacher Materials

* Overhead projector
* Overhead: Learning Log

Student Materials

* A copy of the reading passage for each student
* Learning Log for each student

Lesson Objective

* Students will review information from the reading passage independently.

Teaching Procedures

Reviewing Independently

* Tell students how many minutes they will have to write their summaries in their Learning Logs and set the timer.

* Circulate among students to provide support and assistance, if needed.

* Select students to share the most important information they have learned. You might wish to do this in quick "popcorn" fashion, where one student stands up to share as soon as another sits down. Students don't need to raise their hands, but they do need to pay close attention because only one person can stand to speak at a time.

Frequently Asked Questions About Wrap Up

1. *What should teachers do when students continue to write very low-level and/or simple questions?*

    The purpose of Wrap Up is to give students an opportunity to think intently about the entire passage they have read and to consider what the most important information is in the passage. Although learning to ask and answer simple questions is a part of Wrap Up, eventually teachers will want students to learn to ask questions across levels—including difficult questions. The best way to achieve this is to teach students the components of questions that make them easy or hard and to praise students as they move toward developing more and more challenging questions.

2. *How can teachers help students who form questions directly from the text and do not use their own words?*

    Since the goal is to get students to use their own language to think about what they have read, eventually we want students to move away from question stems or questions taken directly from text and to write their own questions. Initially, however, it may be helpful to provide students with two or more question stems to assist them in writing questions. Then after they have more opportunities to write and hear the questions from fellow students, the number of question stems can be reduced until students are generating all of the questions on their own.

3. *How else can I teach students the difficulty level of questions?*

After students gain confidence and skills in question asking, you can teach students to ask questions that represent a range of difficulty. For example, Ms. Royal taught her students that questions can be categorized as $10 questions—very easy, $20 questions—harder, $30 questions—pretty hard, and $40 questions—very hard. She taught them to consider the following criteria for evaluating questions:

✹ $10 questions are ones where the answer is right in the text and can be provided in one or two words.

✹ $20 questions are ones where the answer is right in the text but requires more than a couple of words to answer it.

✹ $30 questions are ones where the answer is in the text, but you have to search for it in different places. You need to put together information and think to form your answer.

✹ $40 questions are ones where the individual has to use his or her own previous experiences and integrate them with what they have learned from the text.

She provided students with colored paper the size of index cards for recording their questions. She gave them a different color for each level of question. For example $10 questions were always green, $20 questions were always blue, $30 questions were always pink, and $40 questions were always yellow. Thus, depending on the number and color of cards the teacher gave each pair or group, students worked together to generate a question on one side of the card and an answer on the back.

4. *How else can question cards be used?*

Question cards can be used for many activities, including:

✹ as a review activity for groups who complete their work early;

✹ as the source for a Jeopardy game that can be played with the entire class or by a small group;

✹ as questions that will appear on a future test;

✹ as review questions for studying a large section of material; and

✹ as a resource for students who are learning to write good questions.

Putting It All Together

During this session students put all four of the strategies together: Preview, Click and Clunk, Get the Gist, and Wrap Up. At this time students will not be fully proficient users of all four strategies, but they will be familiar enough with them that with support from a partner and the teacher they can use all of them with the same text. Allow 45–50 minutes to complete the activity. Times suggested are approximate—feel free to adjust them for your class depending upon the length and difficulty of the reading passage.

Teacher Materials

* Overhead projector
* Overhead: Learning Log

Student Materials

* A copy of a reading passage for each student (with multiple paragraphs, divided into three sections)
* Learning Log for each student

Lesson Objective

* Students will independently preview a passage, find and figure out clunks, generate main idea statements, write questions, and review information from the reading passage.

Teaching Procedures

* Tell students that today you are going to ask them to work with a partner and to use all four CSR strategies when reading the text. Tell them that you'll be using a timer and they will need to work quickly in order to finish in time.

* When the timer goes off each time, announce to the class what section should be complete and what they should do next.

* While students are working, go from pair to pair to assure that they are completing the designated activity, that all students are participating, and that any problems can be resolved as quickly as possible.

Previewing Independently

* If necessary, review with students the steps you expect them to follow when previewing the text.

* Tell students that they will have six minutes to:
    * Preview the entire passage.
    * Write their notes in their Learning Log.
    * Share their ideas with one another.

* Set the timer.

* Circulate around the room while students are working, providing help or positive reinforcement, and making mental notes about what students are saying.

* When the timer sounds, tell students it is time to move on to reading the passage.

Clicking and Clunking and Getting the Gist Independently

* Tell students how much text you would like them to read before they stop to Click and Clunk and Get the Gist (one or two

paragraphs at a time). If students will be reading two paragraphs at a time, ask them to use their pencils to divide the text into sections, two paragraphs in each section. Tell them that you expect them to find clunks and write a gist for each of the sections.

* Tell them they will have eight minutes to:

  * Read the first section (one or two paragraphs).

  * Write their clunks in their Learning Logs.

  * Use the Fix-up Strategies to figure out what the clunks mean.

  * Write the meanings of the clunks in their Learning Log.

  * Figure out their gists.

  * Share their gists with one another.

* Set the timer.

* Circulate around the room and assist students as necessary, making mental notes of the words that most commonly turn up as clunks.

* After the timer sounds, tell students to continue with the next section of text, even if they haven't quite finished.

* Continue the cycle of reading a paragraph (or two) and having the students Click and Clunk and Get the Gist.

Wrapping Up Independently

* Tell students that they will have six minutes to generate questions about the important ideas in the passage and to answer and discuss the questions. Today, you would like them to write and answer two questions about what they have read.

* Set the timer.

* Circulate around the room while students are working, providing help or positive reinforcement, and noting particularly good questions to return to later or areas needing additional instruction.

* When the timer sounds, tell students it is time to review what they learned and that they will have four minutes to do this.

* Set the timer.

* Circulate around the room providing encouragement and assistance, as needed.

* When the timer sounds, move on to a whole class debriefing.

When the time is up and students have completed Preview, Click and Clunk, Get the Gist, and Wrap Up, it is a good idea to conduct a whole class debriefing for about ten minutes to determine how effective pairs of students were with their previews, clunks, gists, and questions. The teacher uses this opportunity to demonstrate strong strategy use and to provide support and guidance to the class as a whole about how to improve their use and practice of the strategies. The teacher also makes notes of strategies that need to be re-taught or further modeled by the teacher on subsequent days. When students are proficient in applying the strategies on their own or in pairs, they are ready to work in cooperative learning groups. For a description of how to transition students from pairs to small group work, see Chapter 3, "CSR and Cooperative Learning Groups."

References

Klingner, J. K., & S. Vaughn. (2000). The helping behaviors of fifth-graders while using collaborative strategic (CSR) during ESL content classes. *TESOL Quarterly, 34,* 69–98.

Ogle, D. M. (1986). K-W-L: A teaching model that develops active reading of expository text. *The Reading Teacher, 39,* 564–570.

Raphael, T. E. (1982). Question-answering strategies for children. *The Reading Teacher, 36,* 186–190.

Raphael, T. E. (1984). Teaching learners about sources of information for answering comprehension questions. *Journal of Reading, 27,* 303–311.

Raphael, T. E. (1986). Teaching Question-answer relationships revisited. *The Reading Teacher, 39,* 516–522.

Vygotsky, L. S. (1978). *Mind in society: The development of higher psychological processes.* M. Cole, V. John-Steiner, S. Scribner, & E. Souberman, Eds. and Trans. Cambridge, MA: Harvard University Press.

CSR and Cooperative Learning Groups

What is Cooperative Learning?

Cooperative learning occurs when students work together in small groups to accomplish shared goals and to maximize their own and each other's learning. Within cooperative learning groups, students are given two main responsibilities: (a) to assure that they learn the designated material or complete the specified task, and (b) to make sure that all other members of their group do likewise (Johnson & Johnson, 1991).

Typically, cooperative learning groups are small, heterogeneous groups of students. Experts in cooperative learning suggest that group size depends on the nature of the task. We have found that a group size of four students works best for CSR. Group size smaller than three does not provide students with the range of ideas from peers to get the full impact of CSR. Group size larger than five does not give all students the opportunity to be active participants. Groups

Chapter at a Glance

- **What is Cooperative Learning?**

- **Why Should We Include Cooperative Learning?**

- **Components of Cooperative Learning**

- **Assigning Students to Groups**

- **Assigning Roles to Students**

- **Teaching the Roles**

- **The Teacher's Role in Facilitating CSR During Group Work**

- **Cooperative Learning and Classroom Management**

- **Whole Class Activities Before or After Group Work**

are heterogeneous in terms of gender, ethnicity, and reading achievement level. Students are given a structured learning experience to get support from a variety of peers and to share their own strengths as a learner.

In CSR, students discuss the material, help each other understand it, and encourage each other to do their best. Students learn collaborative skills at the same time they are mastering content. They also learn comprehension strategies that are likely to improve their reading comprehension.

Why Should We Include Cooperative Learning?

As you learned in Chapter 1, there are several reasons for including cooperative learning in teaching comprehension reading strategies and for content area learning:

* In comparison with competitive and individualistic methods, cooperative learning has been found to lead to greater academic performance, increased motivation towards learning, increased time on task, improved self-esteem, and more positive social behaviors.

* Cooperative learning fosters the development of higher reasoning and problem-solving skills. This is important for long-term learning and studying. It is also important in preparing for high stakes tests that include higher-order reading comprehension questions.

* Cooperative learning is effective in culturally and linguistically diverse classrooms that include a wide range of achievement levels, and has been recommended by experts in the fields of multicultural education, teaching English as a second language, special education, and general education.

* Through cooperative learning groups, students who represent a range of reading abilities are provided the opportunity to learn strategically and to acquire information from text.

If you think about it, cooperative learning is really a life-long activity. If you work on a volunteer committee or with a team of other professionals at work, you are working in small, heterogeneous groups. Developing the skills to work in positive and constructive ways with others can provide students with tools for succeeding in all walks of life.

The best thing about cooperative learning is that students like it. We surveyed over 500 elementary school students (grades 3–5) to find out what grouping patterns they liked best (Elbaum, Schumm, & Vaughn, 1997). Of six formats included in the survey (whole class, mixed-ability groups, same-ability groups, mixed-ability pairs, same-ability pairs, and independent), mixed-ability groups and pairs were their favorites. We also conducted follow-up interviews with 55 elementary school students (Elbaum, Moody, & Schumm, 1999). Our results were similar; students preferred mixed-ability groups. They did, however, have some suggestions for how best to implement those groups. Their suggestions will be presented later in this chapter in the section entitled, "Cooperative Learning and Classroom Management."

Cooperative learning can be one component of an overall, flexible grouping plan for your classroom (Radencich & McKay,1995). In addition to whole class activities, at times you may want to form same-ability groups for intensive instruction, interest groups for themed projects, and pairs of students for buddy reading and peer tutoring.

We have also used student pairs for Collaborative Strategic Reading. We have found that this procedure works especially well with students in younger grades.

Components of Cooperative Learning

But I already have my students working in groups. How is this different?

Perhaps the most frequently implemented seating arrangement in elementary classrooms today is the placement of students in some type of group arrangement. Teachers often use these seating arrangements to allow better performing students to assist students who need help. While this is often a useful practice, it is not a cooperative learning group. Cooperative learning groups involve more than just placing students in a group and telling them to work together. Nor is it having students sit side-by-side, with the one who finishes first helping the slower student. Cooperative learning consists of planned and organized group work where students have a specific function in the group and all students acquire knowledge and skills. According to Johnson and Johnson (1991), five basic elements must be included for a lesson to be cooperative:

* The first is **positive interdependence**. In other words, it involves students believing they must "sink or swim" together. Students need to think that their work benefits others in the group, and that their teammate's work benefits them. One way teachers can structure positive interdependence is by assigning complementary roles to students.

* For the benefits of cooperative learning to be maximized, there must be considerable face-to-face, **promoting interaction** among students. Group members need to encourage, support, and assist each other's efforts to learn. It is important for students to learn to explain their reasoning to each other.

* The third element is **individual accountability**. This exists when student performance is assessed regularly. Group members should perceive that they must fulfill their responsibilities in order for each individual and the group to be successful. One way to achieve this is to require students to certify that each group member can correctly explain the answers, and then to randomly select one member of the group to explain the group's answers (i.e., using "Numbered Heads Together"[1]). Another way to promote individual accountability is to have students complete individual learning logs (Chapter 4).

* Fourth, **social skills** must be taught. Learning groups are not productive unless members are skilled in cooperating with each other. Teachers need to carefully define and model appropriate group behaviors. These behaviors should be practiced, using simulation and role playing, and continually monitored and reinforced. Teach one social skill at a time, posting each behavior on a chart for reference as it is learned. Some of the skills students learn are how to: (a) listen attentively, (b) ask clarifying questions, (c) take turns speaking, (d) provide positive feedback, and (e) resolve conflicts.

* Finally, at the end of each cooperative learning session, students should **evaluate** how well they worked together by answering two questions: (a) what is something each member did that was helpful for the group? and (b) what is something each member could do to make the group even better next time?

---

[1] *Numbered Heads Together* (Kagan, 1990): This is a cooperative learning technique used for review and for checking understanding. In their groups, students are each assigned a number. The teacher asks a question; students then consult in their groups to make sure everyone knows the answer. The teacher then calls upon one student to answer (e.g., a "number one," or a "number four"). Students do not know ahead of time which number will be called.

How can I implement cooperative learning groups in my classroom?

Think about the activities and assignments that are already part of your teaching routine. Which of these activities would be suitable for implementation following the components of cooperative groups described above? Implement cooperative learning groups several times a week. Students who are already familiar with working in cooperative groups are much more successful when learning CSR.

Assigning Students to Groups

CSR involves three components: (1) learning comprehension strategies, (2) learning to work together in groups, and (3) learning content material to prepare for class discussions and tests. WHEW! That's a great deal to put together. For many students, it's like rubbing your stomach and patting your head—at the same time! Because this is a complex learning task, group composition is critical.

In some cases, teachers let students select their own groups. For some learning tasks, that might be appropriate. For CSR, teachers tell us that students need to be assigned to groups. If possible, students should sit in their groups throughout the day, with their desks arranged together.

The following procedure may be useful to you as you establish your CSR groups. The procedure is designed for group sizes of four students but could be used with any group size.

* **Step 1: Rank students by achievement.** List all of the students in your class, starting with the highest achiever and finishing with the lowest achiever. To determine achievement levels, use recent test scores, past grades, or the knowledge you have about students' reading levels. You can do this relatively quickly since the purpose is to assure that you do not have all of the strong readers or weak readers in any one CSR group.

* **Step 2: Identify your leaders.** Put a star next to the names of students who are able

to lead a group. You will want to be sure that you have at least one leader in each of your CSR groups. Note, however, that the structure of CSR helps all students be successful in the role of leader.

* **Step 3: Select the first group.** Choose the top, bottom, and two middle students from your class list. Assign these students to group one, unless (a) they are all the same gender, (b) they do not reflect the ethnic composition of the class, (c) they are worst enemies, or (d) they are best friends. If any of these are the case, readjust the group by moving up or down one student on the list. Now, pick a leader from the group, considering who the members are and how you can best balance group composition.

* **Step 4: Select the remaining groups.** To produce the second group, repeat Step 2. Continue until all students have been assigned to a group. Create groups of five if there are any remaining students. After using the procedure above, review the composition of each group. Think about whether each group can work together as a team. If you see potential problems, then make adjustments.

What happens when a student is absent?

Some teachers select a student with good social and academic skills as a "floater" to fill in when students are absent. If a student is absent consistently, then that student's group may have five members to remedy the problem of frequent absences. Most teachers assign the role of the absent student to another student in the group and the group functions very well with just three students.

How often should group composition be adjusted?

This varies somewhat by teacher and class, but the following suggestions have worked for many teachers. First, when starting CSR we suggest that students remain in the same group for about nine weeks. They are learning their roles and responsibilities and it takes some time for the group to learn to "click" and to work together well. Of course, if there are particular students who are not working well in a group, we suggest that they be shifted. After groups are functioning well, the teacher needs to decide which students or entire groups would benefit from rotating students. Some teachers have a particular group that is working so well she is unwilling to break them up. Other teachers find that rotating groups from time to time can solve the problem of "I don't want to work with him or her." The arrival of a new student in the class can be used as a reason for disbanding a group that is not working well. Often, despite any initial problems, the students in a group start to depend on each other to provide support on homework and other classwork as well as CSR activities.

One teacher who changes groups more frequently, every four or five weeks, noted, "Revisiting group assignments periodically keeps learners excited about the process and also assists in socializing all students. When students have the opportunity to work with everyone in the class at one time or another, it fosters a more defined class identity and improves overall cooperation" (Juan Cabrera, fourth-grade teacher).

Assigning Roles to Students

Essential to the success of cooperative learning groups is the premise that each student in the group has a meaningful role that contributes to the overall success of the group. Before students in your class implement CSR, they should have multiple opportunities to implement and experience cooperative learning groups in which they have assigned roles, understand the features and expectations of those assigned roles, and become experts in at least one of the assigned roles (see section below for list of assigned roles). Some teachers like to keep students in the same role for several weeks, at least four, so that he/she has adequate time to practice and rehearse the expectations and skills associated with that role. This way, when roles are reassigned within the group, each member of the group is an expert at

a particular role. After students have had sufficient time to practice and rehearse a single role, they can then alternate roles more frequently. It is important to ensure that all students experience a variety of roles and that every student has an opportunity to be the leader. Ms. Royal says, "I think it is very important that students demonstrate that they are an expert in the role they are assigned. Thus, I practice with groups of students who are going to be responsible for 'click and clunk' or 'gist' or any of the strategies to assure that they can really be the leaders on those strategies." Ms. Royal spends 10–15 minutes with all of the students who are serving in a particular role (e.g., all of the leaders) and assures that they know what they are doing and how to proceed. She believes that these students then teach the others in the group how to "perform" their role. This way, when students are assigned to serve in a different role they have acquired the skills to do so.

Possible Roles That Can Be Used in CSR Cooperative Groups

If you have used cooperative learning in the past, you are aware that there are multiple possibilities for roles that students can assume. For CSR to function smoothly, at least three roles are essential, **leader, clunk expert**, and **gist expert**. Other roles (**encourager, announcer, timekeeper**) require fewer skills. Roles such as encourager, announcer, and time keeper can also be multiply assigned. Thus, if you prefer to have students work in groups of three, one student can be the leader and encourager, another student the clunk expert and announcer, and the third student the gist expert and timekeeper.

In this section, possible roles will be described. You can use these descriptions to teach your students about the role they will play in the group and the responsibilities associated with their role. Some teachers actually tape a description of the role and its responsibilities to the inside of a manila folder. When students assume a role, they are given the manila folder as a reminder of their duties and responsibilities. Cue cards or sheets for various roles are included in Chapter 4.

Leader

Your Role

The leader guides the group in the use of the four strategies: (1) Preview, (2) Click and Clunk, (3) Get the Gist, and (4) Wrap Up. This role is very important because the Leader reminds group members when to do their jobs and helps the group stay on track.

Your Responsibilities

* Use the Leader's cue card to prompt group members about the four strategies.

* Use the Leader's cue card to prompt other students when to do their jobs.

* Remind the group to stay on task. Talk only to group members and talk only about the strategies and the reading assignment.

Announcer

Your Role

The announcer calls on students to share their ideas and makes sure that each member of the group participates in CSR.

Your Responsibilities

* When the leader tells you, call on different group members to read or share an idea.

* Make sure that all group members have a chance to talk and that one group member does not talk too much.

* Remind your group that only one person talks at a time.

Clunk Expert

Your Role

The clunk expert helps the group members figure out words they don't understand. This is an important job because the clunk expert helps group members clarify any misunderstandings they may have.

Your Responsibilities

* Ask any group members if they have clunks.

* Ask if anyone knows the meaning of the clunk.

* Use the Clunk Expert's Cue Cards to help figure out clunks no one knows.

* Summarize the meaning of the clunk for your group so that each person can write the meaning in their Learning Logs.

Gist Expert

Your Role

The gist expert works with the group to decide on the best gist for each section of the reading assignment. This is an important role because the gist expert helps the group decide on the main idea for each section.

Your Responsibilities

* Ask students to write their gists in their learning logs.

* After the announcer calls on someone to share a gist, ask the group if they agree.

* Work with your group to decide on the best gist.

Encourager

Your Role

The encourager watches the group and lets group members know when they do something well. This role is very important because the encourager helps all members feel part of the group and feel good about the contributions they make.

Your Responsibilities

* Watch each member of the group.

* Use the Encourager's Cue Card to help you think of good things to say about: (1) how your group worked together and (2) how the group helped each other learn.

* Use the Encourager's Cue Card to help your group discuss things that will help the group work better together.

Timekeeper

Your Role

The timekeeper helps the group complete the reading assignment in a timely way. This is an important role because the timekeeper helps the group make the best use of class time.

Your Responsibilities

* Set the timer for each portion of CSR. The leader will tell you when to begin.

* Let the leader and other members of the group know when it is time to move on.

Teaching the Roles

The best way for students to learn their roles is for the teacher to form "expert" groups. Pull all the students who are going to assume the role of leader together. Explain to them the importance of their role and how they will interact with other students in the group. Next, review their responsibilities and model how they should implement them.

Provide each student with an opportunity to practice the role and allow other students to give feedback. Continue this practice with each "expert" group until all students know and have had an opportunity to demonstrate successfully how they would implement their role.

We suggest that you teach students their roles through the use of cue cards (Chapter 4). Cue cards can be useful when they are used to outline the procedures to be followed in cooperative learning groups and to provide structure and support for students while they are learning to apply the comprehension strategies. They help students to stay focused and on task. Each role has a corresponding cue card that explains the steps to be followed to carry out the role.

The next step is to put all of the roles together. Pull together one cooperative learning group that includes students representing all roles. Work with this group to develop proficiency in intertwining their roles. When they have developed a certain level of proficiency, have them demonstrate to the rest of the class. We call this a "fish bowl" because the group sits in front of the class for the demonstration.

Taking the time to teach the roles and teach how the roles interact is worth the time and effort. When students feel comfortable with their roles, they have more energy to concentrate on the strategies and on the content they are learning. Mrs. Sullivan explains, "although it seems like you are spending a lot of time teaching roles and responsibilities early on, I can assure you the payoff is enormous."

Most teachers find it is helpful to "listen in" on a CSR group so that they can get some idea of how the group can be expected to function. Following is a sample lesson that occurred as part of a CSR group in a fifth-grade class. Listen to how carefully these students work to assure that all youngsters are learning and participating in the group. We are confident that your students can have the same successes.

Sample CSR Lesson

Preview

Brainstorm

Leader: *We know that today's topic is the skeletal system. Let's brainstorm and write everything we already know about the topic in our learning logs. Timekeeper, please start the timer.*

[Timekeeper starts the timer that has been set for one and a half minutes. Everyone writes quietly in their Learning Logs until the timer goes off.]

Timekeeper: *Time's up.*

Leader: *OK, who would like to share their best ideas? Announcer, please call on two people to share.*

Announcer: *John?*

John: *I already know that the muscular system works with the skeletal system to get our bodies to move.*

Encourager: *Good answer.*

Announcer: *Pablo?*

Pablo: *Umm, I know that the skeletal system is made up of different kinds of bones.*

Predict

Leader: *Now let's predict. Look at the title, pictures, and headings and think about what we might learn today. Write your ideas in your learning logs. Timekeeper, start the timer.*

[Timekeeper starts the timer that has been set for one and a half minutes. Everyone writes quietly in their Learning Logs until the timer goes off.]

Timekeeper: *Time's up.*

Students' Roles:

Tasha = Leader

Julia = Announcer

Rosemary = Encourager and Timekeeper

John = Clunk Expert

Pablo = Gist Expert

Note that Pablo is a student with learning disabilities.

Leader: *OK, who would like to share their best ideas? Announcer, please call on two people to share.*

Announcer: *Rosemary.*

Rosemary: *I think we are going to learn about where the bones are and the places of the bones and their names and what we use them for.*

Announcer: *OK, I'm calling on myself.*

Julia: *I predict that we'll learn how the bones of the skeletal system connect.*

Encourager: *Good prediction.*

Read

Leader: *OK, who would like to read the first paragraph?*

Announcer: *Rosemary?*

Rosemary (reading aloud): *How can you keep all the muscles healthy? Without healthy bones and muscles even simple actions would not be possible. One way to keep bones and muscles healthy is to eat the foods shown here. Diary products, fruits, and vegetables contain calcium and other minerals. Remember that calcium helps make bones hard and strong. Calcium is also used by muscles when they contract. Milk, fish, and eggs contain proteins. Proteins help build muscle tissue. Bread and cereals provide energy that muscles need to move bones. Which of these foods have you eaten today?*

Click and Clunk

Leader: *Did everyone understand what we read? If you didn't, write your clunks in your Learning Log. Announcer, please call on someone to say their clunk.*

Announcer: *Pablo.*

Pablo: *Calcium.*

Leader: *Clunk Expert, please help us out.*

Clunk Expert: *Read the sentence again and think about what would make sense. Try to get a clue. Think if you see any other words that can help you. Did you get anything?*

Pablo: *No.*

Clunk Expert: *OK, now I do, I get something. It is a mineral. Do you know what 'mineral' is?*

Pablo: *Yeah.*

Clunk Expert: *What is it?*

Pablo: *It's like a kind of vitamin.*

Clunk Expert: *OK, calcium is a type of element that there is in the bones. And, the bones need that. Calcium helps the bones in order to make them strong. Do you now understand what calcium is?*

Pablo: *Yes.*

Clunk Expert: *What is it again, one more time?*

Pablo: *It is a type of element that helps the bones grow.*

Clunk Expert: *OK, good.*

Leader: *Any more clunks?*

Group: *No.*

Get the Gist

Leader: *It's time to Get the Gist. Gist Expert, please help us out.*

Gist Expert: *What is the most important idea we have learned about the topic so far? Everyone write a gist in your Learning Log. Timekeeper, please set the timer for one minute.*

[The timekeeper sets the timer. Everyone writes quietly until the timer goes off.]

Gist Expert: *Who has a gist to share?*

Announcer: *Rosemary, can you please answer that?*

Rosemary: *Calcium helps make bones and teeth strong.*

Announcer: *OK, does everyone agree with that answer? John?*

John: *I think the gist is that it's important to eat healthy foods to keep our muscles and bones healthy.*

Gist Expert: *I think that's it.*

Read

Leader: *OK, who would like to read the next paragraph?*

Announcer: *John.*

John (reading): *A second way to keep bones and muscles healthy is to exercise. Exercise helps bones and muscles become stronger. Strong skeletal muscles move bones more easily. Exercise also helps make heart muscles stronger. Many kinds of sports and play are good exercise. These children are getting another kind of exercise that helps keep bones and muscles healthy. What kind of exercise have you done today?*

Click and Clunk

Leader: *Does anybody have a clunk?*

Group: *No.*

Get the Gist

Leader: *OK, then it's time to Get the Gist. Gist Expert, please help us out.*

Gist Expert: *What is the most important idea we have learned about the topic so far? Everyone write a gist in your Learning Log. Timekeeper, please set the timer for one minute.*

[The timekeeper sets the timer. Everyone writes quietly until the timer goes off.]

Gist Expert: *Who has a gist to share?*

Announcer: *Tasha.*

Tasha: *Exercise helps bones and muscles become strong.*

Gist Expert: *Does everyone agree? Me too, I think that's right.*

Read

Leader: *Who would like to read the next paragraph?*

Announcer: *I call on myself.*

Julia (reading): *A third way to keep bones and muscles healthy is to rest and sleep. When you exercise muscles you are using energy that is released from food. As this energy is released, waste materials are formed. This makes bones and muscles feel tired. When you rest, your waste materials are carried away from the muscles by your blood. Rest also gives the body time to make and repair bone and muscle tissue.*

Click and Clunk

Leader: *Does anybody have a clunk?*

Group: *No.*

Get the Gist

Leader: *It's time to Get the Gist. Gist Expert, please help us out.*

Gist Expert: *What is the most important idea we have learned about the topic so far? Everyone write a gist in your Learning Log. Timekeeper, please set the timer for one minute.*

[The timekeeper sets the timer. Everyone writes quietly until the timer goes off.]

Gist Expert: *Who has a gist to share?*

Announcer: *John.*

John: *When you exercise, muscles use energy that is released from food.*

Gist Expert: *Does everyone agree?*

Announcer: *I think it's that we need rest and sleep to keep healthy. Rosemary?*

Rosemary: *We need to rest because our muscles get tired when they use energy.*

Gist Expert: *I think that's good.*

Read

Leader: *Who would like to read the next paragraph?*

Announcer: *Pablo.*

Pablo (reading, with help from his peers): *What are some problems with bones? Bones are strong, but they can be injured. Have you ever broken a bone? Because most young people are very active, they may break bones. A crack or break in a* bone is called a fracture. The picture shows bones and fractures in two different ways. In an open fracture, the ends of the broken bone stick out. In a closed fracture, the bone is broken but the ends of the bone do not stick out. Which fracture is probably more dangerous? Because bones are made of living tissues they can repair themselves.

Click and Clunk

Leader: *Does anybody have a clunk? OK, please write your clunks in your Learning Logs.*

Announcer: *Rosemary?*

Rosemary: *Fractured.*

Leader: *Clunk Expert, please help us out.*

Clunk Expert: *Does anyone know what 'fractured' means? Tasha?*

Tasha: *It says right here in the paragraph that a fracture is a crack or break in the bone. Have you ever broken a bone? This picture shows you. This is a fractured bone, OK?*

Rosemary: *OK.*

Get the Gist

Leader: *It's time to Get the Gist. Gist Expert, please help us out.*

Gist Expert: *What is the most important idea we have learned about the topic so far? Everyone write a gist in your Learning Log. Timekeeper, please set the timer for one minute.*

[The timekeeper sets the timer. Everyone writes quietly until the timer goes off.]

Gist Expert: *Who has a gist to share?*

Announcer: *John?*

John: *A break in a bone is called a fracture.*

Gist Expert: *OK, can you add to that?*

John: *Yes, it is trying to say that when you break your bone you can have a closed fracture or an open fracture.*

Encourager: *Good job.*

Wrap Up

Generating and Answering Questions

Leader: *Now let's think of some questions to check if we really understood what we read. Remember to start your questions with who, when, what, where, why, or how. Everyone write your questions in your Learning Log. Timekeeper, please set the timer for three minutes.*

[Timekeeper sets the timer. Everyone writes quietly until the timer goes off.]

Leader: *Who would like to share their best question? Announcer, please call on someone.*

Announcer: *Tasha.*

Tasha: *What might happen if your bones did not contain enough calcium?*

Pablo: *They will break.*

Tasha: *OK, they will probably break. But can we add a little bit?*

Rosemary: *Well, first of all, what is calcium? And then we can figure out what it says and how it helps the bones.*

Pablo: *OK, calcium is something that keeps the bones healthy.*

Announcer: *Tasha?*

Tasha: *If you don't have enough calcium, then the bones will get weak and break. And, then after you die, your bones decay and you* *turn into dust. Your bones will, like, decompose in your body.*

Pablo: *OK, I would say the same thing because the bones without calcium are nothing.*

Leader: *Who else has a question?*

Encourager: *Wait, that was a good job answering that question.*

Leader: *OK, now . . .*

Announcer: *I have a question. How could we keep muscles healthy? Rosemary?*

Rosemary: *By eating grains, cereal, dairy products like milk, meat, fish, and bread, and chicken.*

Julia: *Yeah, and also by getting exercise and enough rest.*

Leader: *Good, anyone else?*

Announcer: *John.*

John: *How does rest make you healthy after exercise?*

Leader: *Please call on someone to answer the question.*

Announcer: *I'll answer it. When you exercise your muscles, you use energy that is released from food. Resting allows the body to save up more energy, and also to repair muscle and bone tissue.*

Encourager: *Great answer.*

Review

Leader: *It's time to review. We will have one and a half minutes to write what we learned in our Learning Logs. Timekeeper, start the timer.*

[The timekeeper sets the timer and everyone works quietly until it goes off.]

Leader: *Now let's go around the group and each say something that we learned. Announcer, call on someone to start.*

Announcer: *Rosemary.*

Rosemary: *I learned different ways to keep my muscles and bones healthy.*

Pablo: *I learned that bones need calcium to be healthy.*

John: *I learned that rest is really important so that your body can store up energy.*

Julia: *I learned that there are two kinds of fractures, open fractures and closed fractures.*

Tasha: *Bones are living tissues, so they can repair themselves.*

Compliments and Suggestions

Leader: *The Encourager has been watching carefully and will now tell us two things we did really well as a group today.*

Encourager: *I think we did a really good job taking turns today and not interrupting each other. Also, everyone participated.*

Leader: *Is there anything that would help us do even better next time?*

Encourager: *Well, I think we could still do a better job using "six-inch voices"[2] so that we don't get too loud.*

Leader: *Anything else?*

Encourager: *No, I don't think so.*

Leader: *OK, thank you. That's a wrap!*

---

[2] "Six-Inch Voices": Students learn to use different sized voices for different situations. A "two-inch voice" is used for talking very quietly only with a neighbor. "Six-inch voices" are appropriate for small groups. Students talk in "twelve-inch voices" when in larger groups. Practicing this helps with volume control.

These students stopped after every paragraph to Click and Clunk and Get the Gist. You might want to have your students read two paragraphs at a time instead so that the lesson proceeds a little more quickly. Also, in this class the teacher did not have students keep track of points, but you may wish to do so. This group included five students (in this class some groups consisted of four members while others had five). It is possible to have groups with smaller numbers of participants whereby one student plays more than one role. It is easy to combine the roles of the Announcer and Encourager, or Announcer and Gist Expert, for example.

The Teacher's Role in Facilitating CSR During Group Work

When students are implementing CSR within their small groups, the teacher's role is to facilitate students' success. There are several tips that teachers can implement to assure that they are maximizing students' performance during their group work.

1. **Spend extended time with each group at least once every two weeks.** Spend at least 20 minutes with each group on a regular basis. During this time assure that students are implementing their roles effectively, that groups are spending a minimal amount of time on "management" and a maximum amount of time on reading and thinking about what they read. This is also an excellent opportunity for the teacher to "role play" the roles of one or more of the students to demonstrate how they can work as well as possible. The teacher can also spend extended time in a group to demonstrate to the class a procedure that a group is using that is effective and that can be modeled by other groups.

2. **Monitor the performance of each group.** In addition to spending extended time each session with one group, it is important to move from group to group, spending three to five minutes with each. During this time the teacher can: (a) monitor the learning logs of the group to assure that students are actively participating in all of the strategies and using them effectively, (b) check the definitions students have written for their "clunks" to assure that they are accurate, (c) help groups with "clunks" that they have not been able to resolve so that understanding the text is easier for them, (d) check the gists they've written and provide feedback on them, (e) check the performance of group members to assure that everyone is participating, and (f) make mental and/or written notes of students' clunks and gists to discuss during a whole class wrap up (e.g., "I noticed that a lot of you had trouble with the word 'economy'; Group 2 came up with a really good definition. Would you please share it?").

3. **Monitor the performance of each student within the group.** One of the more challenging but important roles of the teacher while students are working in small groups is to assure that all members of the group are active participants who are both contributing and learning from the group's efforts. Most teachers are aware that there are selected students who are quite able to "take over" a group and whose ideas and work dominate the group. It is very important to assure that all members of the group are contributing to all aspects of CSR including Preview, Get the Gist, Click and Clunk, and Wrap Up.

4. **Highlight the performance of students or groups who are implementing the strategies exceedingly well.** By moving from group to group and spending extended time with one group

during each session the teacher is able to keep "tabs" on the performance of the groups and individuals within the groups. Furthermore, the teacher obtains information about how groups are performing. The teacher can assist other groups by sharing this information with the class.

What Would You Do If You Heard This?

The following situations were taken from transcripts of actual Collaborative Strategic Reading sessions.

* **Situation 1**: What would you say to this group? (Note that "people that serve on the little things" is unclear and incomplete, but the group leader moves on to the next step anyway.)

  Leader: What do we think we will find out about the topic?

  Teresa: It's going to be about people, and how they go to the attractions (in Orlando). (This is an accurate prediction.)

  Jenny: People that serve on the little things?

  Leader: OK, who would like to read?

* **Situation 2**: What would you say to this group? (Note that the clunk has been defined inaccurately.)

  Randy: I have a clunk. It's "restored."

  Clunk Expert: Does anyone know what "restored" means?

  Announcer: Manny?

  Manny: It's sort of like when you have a big warehouse and you store things there, I think.

  Randy: So it's stuff that's been stored again?

  Manny: Yeah, because "re" means to do it again.

Cooperative Learning and Classroom Management

Earlier in this chapter we mentioned that we conducted interviews of elementary school students to learn what they think about mixed-ability groups (Elbaum, Moody, & Schumm, 1999). We learned that students generally like working in groups. However, they did express the following concerns:

* Sometimes it gets too noisy in the classroom.

* The teacher doesn't always get around to helping you in the group.

* Students who are low achieving get embarrassed when they can't participate at the same level with their peers.

Interestingly, classroom teachers frequently share these same concerns. Here are some techniques we have learned from CSR teachers who have overcome these obstacles.

Classroom Noise

Assigning students specific roles will go a long way in promoting positive student interaction. However, just because your students are working in groups, don't forget your regular behavior management plan. Remember to reinforce the rules and consequences you have already established.

Set a few rules specifically for CSR—not many, just a few that students will remember and that you will enforce consistently.

Rules for Collaborative Strategic Reading

1. Talk only to the members of your group.

2. Talk only about CSR.

3. Use six-inch voices.

4. When you have a question, have the Leader raise his or her hand to get help from the teacher.

One teacher we know worked in a small, portable classroom. To keep the noise level under control, she issued each student in the cooperative learning group 15 poker chips. Students could only speak when they placed a poker chip in the middle of the table. This system encouraged students to speak one at a time. Also, it helped teachers monitor who was not participating and who was monopolizing the discussion.

Another teacher provided each group with a pretend microphone. Members of the group could only talk when the leader gave them the microphone.

Providing Support to Groups

Even after you spend time teaching the roles, students will still need your help in mastering their roles, developing proficiency with the strategies, and learning the content. Be prepared to provide support and to teach when necessary. As you circulate among groups, it is helpful to take notes about student questions and concerns about content and procedures. When you have a whole class Wrap Up at the end, you can use your notes for a follow up.

Supporting Low-Achieving Students

One of the most important lessons of CSR is teaching students how to work with a variety of peers in positive ways. Having a "no tolerance" position on ridicule is imperative. In addition, students need to be taught how to provide criticisms in constructive ways.

Elbaum, Moody, and Schumm (1999, p. 65) suggest the following:

Teaching Students the Three Rules of Constructive Criticism

Focus on the behavior, not the person. Let's say a member of your group skips over some words when she is reading aloud. If you say, "You messed up!" or "You didn't read that right!" that just makes the person feel bad and doesn't give her any help. Instead, you can tell the person what she did: "You skipped over some words." That will give her an idea of how she can do better the next time.

Be specific. Take the example of the student who skipped over some words when she was reading. She probably doesn't know which words she skipped! So it would be even *more* helpful to say, "You left out three words [here you say what the words were] in the middle of the second sentence."

Say what's good, not just what's bad. Tell other students what they did *well*—not just what they didn't do so well! Take the example of the student who skipped over some words again. You could say, "Even though you skipped over some words in the second sentence, you read all the other sentences without skipping anything and you used a lot of expression." That would let her know that she did something well and would encourage her to keep trying.

Low-achieving students, students with learning disabilities, and students who are English language learners are frequently afraid to take risks. Setting a supportive environment for risk-taking is crucial. Talk with students about taking risks and "just giving it a good try." Also, talk with students about appropriate ways to respond when a group member makes a mistake. We have learned that students *do* learn to take risks when they are encouraged to do so by their peers and when group members are understanding when someone makes a mistake.

Whole Class Activities Before or After Group Work

Even when students are working effectively within their groups, whole class activities are an excellent way to provide additional instruction, enhance knowledge and strategy use, and highlight key aspects of CSR that allow students to be even more effective within their groups. Many teachers conduct a whole class introduction when beginning a new unit or chapter in a content area textbook. Teachers also frequently conduct a whole class Wrap Up.

Frequently Asked Questions

1. *When students are working in groups, do I ever do any whole class CSR work again?*

   We believe that reserving a few minutes for a whole class activity before and/or after students use CSR in their groups (depending upon the skills you would like to emphasize) is a very good idea. Since CSR is time consuming, it is important to designate a specified amount of time, albeit usually short, to provide a preview or follow-up whole class activity. These whole class activities can range from 10 minutes to 30 minutes depending upon the nature of the instruction or support provided by the teacher.

2. *What types of whole class activities can I do before I ask students to work in their groups?*

   There are many effective mini-lessons that can be conducted prior to students working in groups. Remember, you do not need to teach a mini-lesson prior to every CSR group work session. Some examples of mini-lessons prior to small group CSR:

   ❋ Conduct the Preview as a whole class activity rather than asking students to do it in their small groups. Practicing it

as a whole class reminds students how to effectively use the strategies. Also, whole class Previews may be particularly effective when the passage to be read is on a brand new topic about which students have little background knowledge.

   ❋ Identify the clunks that you think most students will have in the text. Pre-teach the clunks so that students can spend less time on this activity while they are reading.

   ❋ Provide students with three question stems to assist them in writing their Wrap Up questions.

   ❋ Review the role of one or more of the students in the group to assure that they are all contributing as effectively as possible.

3. *What types of whole class activities can I do after I ask students to work in their groups?*

   Perhaps one of the most frequent challenges teachers have faced when using CSR is that once students are in their groups and working effectively, they allow them to work like this the entire time and do not reserve time at the end for whole class activities. Like activities prior to CSR group work, it is not necessary to save time for whole class activities following every CSR group work lesson; however, it is important to do it frequently. Following are some examples of activities that can be used effectively following CSR group work:

   ❋ Ask a representative from each group to provide the clunks their group encountered. List the clunks on the board and demonstrate for students how much overlap there was across groups. Discuss the clunks that were identified by more than one group. Ask students to tell how they figured out what the clunk meant. Discuss whether the clunk has more than one meaning.

✳ Again using clunks, make a list of all of the clunks identified by the groups. Ask groups who did not identify a clunk that was identified by another group to put their heads together for one minute and then to explain the clunk to the class. This gives students opportunities to teach but also holds them accountable, so that they can not "slip by" without identifying clunks that they really have.

✳ Ask a representative from each group to tell you their gist for the first section of the passage. Compare gists. Discuss which aspects of each of the gists are strong and which aspects could use improvement. Give each group a chance to revise their gist. Ask them to state them again and provide feedback when positive changes were made.

✳ Ask students to tell the class whether they made any predictions that were *not* accurate. After reading the passage, ask them how they would now revise their prediction. Ask students to tell the class whether they made any predictions that were accurate. Ask them to describe the information that they used to make the prediction.

✳ The questions from Wrap Up provide many opportunities for whole-class activities. For example, each group can identify one question that they ask the class as a whole. They then select a student from a group to answer the question. The group is given 30 seconds to confer to decide their answer and then the selected student reports for the group. If the answer is correct, the group the student represents gets one point. If the answer is incorrect, the point goes to the group that asked the question. If the teacher is using color cards to represent question diffi-

culty, the class can play games such as Jeopardy or Millionaire to see who can earn the most money. The teacher can also use Wrap Up to teach students more challenging questions and question types.

CSR Follow-Up Activities

Bilingual Dictionaries: English language learners write their clunks with definitions in English and their native language, and add illustrations.

Bulletin Board: Each student writes a clunk and a sentence that demonstrates the meaning of the clunk on a large index card, with a picture. These can be arranged on a bulletin board entitled "From Clunks to Clicks."

Clunk Books: Students create flip books that include clunks and illustrations that represent their meanings.

Clunk Concentration: Students use small index cards. On one card they write a clunk and on another the definition. These can be used to play concentration with a partner or a small group.

Crossword Puzzles: Students develop a crossword puzzle using the clunks or other key words related to the topic. The puzzle can then be shared with other group members, or passed along to another group.

Mnemonic Devices: Students apply memory strategies to help them remember what they have learned. Students might create a rhyme (e.g., "In 1492, Columbus sailed the ocean blue."), an acronym (e.g., "HOMES" to represent each of the Great Lakes), or a spatial layout (i.e., given a list of items to be remembered, students mentally place each item in a different room of their house; to recall the items they retrace their steps and retrieve each item from where it was placed).

Numbered Heads Together: Students in each group number off from 1–4 or 1–5 (depending upon how many students are in each group). The teacher asks a review question. Students in each group then "put their heads together" to discuss the question and make sure that everyone in the group knows the answer. The teacher then rolls two dice. The number on one die indicates which group is selected; the number on the second die indicates which student within the group answers the question.

Quizzes: Each group writes their best question on the board and the class then answers all of the questions as a homework or in-class assignment.

Send A Problem: Each group selects the best question they have generated and passes that question to a different group to answer.

Theme Pictures: Students draw pictures about the topic that was just read. Throughout the picture they then write key words about the topic that correspond with their illustrations.

Venn Diagrams: Each group draws two large intersecting circles on a paper or an overhead transparency. First, students compare two different ideas by generating a list of similarities and writing these in the overlapping portion of the circles. Then, they contrast the two ideas, and write differences in the two portions of the circles that are not connected.

Web: Students categorize words or ideas and place these in a semantic map that visually represents the relationships among ideas. Students write the topic in a circle in the middle of the paper, and then write related words in categories arranged around the topic.

References

Elbaum, B., S. W. Moody, & J. S. Schumm. (1999). Mixed-ability grouping for reading: What students think. *Learning Disabilities Research and Practice, 14,* 61–66.

Elbaum, B., J. S. Schumm, & S. Vaughn. (1997). Urban middle-elementary students' perceptions of grouping formats for reading instruction. *Elementary School Journal, 97,* 475–500.

Johnson, D. W., & R. T. Johnson. (1991). *Learning together and alone: Cooperative, competitive, and individualistic learning* (3rd ed.). Boston: Allyn & Bacon.

Kagen, S. (1990). *Cooperative learning resources for teachers.* San Juan Capistrano, CA: Resources for Teachers.

Radencich, M., & L. McKay. (1995). *Flexible grouping for literacy in the elementary grades.* Needham, MA: Allyn & Bacon.

CSR Materials

Various materials are required for Collaborative Strategic Reading. We suggest that you keep readily available enough sets of materials for each of your CSR groups. Some teachers use plastic baskets for this purpose. Others use folders or plastic file boxes.

Reading Materials

We designed CSR primarily for the expository text found in content area textbooks. It can also be used with narrative text, although the Reciprocal Teaching comprehension strategies are probably better suited for narrative stories. CSR is meant to replace whole class read-the-chapter-and-answer-the-questions-at-the-back work, not hands on, inquiry-based, research, or other types of instruction. CSR can, however, be used effectively with other reading materials.

Content Area Textbooks

Although CSR will "work" with any expository text students might be expected to read, some textbooks lend themselves to strategy implementation more than others. It is very important to examine your social studies or science series to determine which is the most appropriate for CSR. Many texts seem to be dense with new vocabulary words and little context that might provide clues to the reader. Some texts list facts with little regard for telling a coherent, meaningful story. If possible, select a book with well-formed, interesting passages that are conducive

Chapter at a Glance

- **Reading Materials**
- **CSR Learning Logs**
- **CSR Cue Cards and Sheets**
- **CSR Clunk Cards**
- **Timer**
- **Score Cards**

to strategy application. Such text is characterized by: (a) clues that help students predict what they will be learning, (b) definitions for key vocabulary built into the text, (c) one main idea in a paragraph with relevant supporting details, and (d) context that helps students connect new information with prior knowledge. If you place two textbooks side by side, you can often readily see the differences.

Non-Fiction Magazines

Many teachers like to use CSR with the *Weekly Reader*, *Scholastic Magazine*, *Teen Newsweek*, or similar non-fiction publications to which their school subscribes. These magazines have brief articles that capture students' interest and can be read in a short time. We have found the *Weekly Reader* to be excellent for teaching CSR. The articles tend to be easier to comprehend than those in textbooks and lend themselves well to strategy application. Also, because they are often about a current news topic, they tend to inspire interesting discussions. Once students have mastered the CSR strategies and are comfortable working in their cooperative learning groups, they can be introduced to a more difficult textbook. We know teachers who continue to use the *Weekly Reader* even after their students are proficient with CSR. They regularly use CSR with their textbooks twice a week, and also have students implement CSR when reading the *Weekly Reader* on Friday afternoons. Some teachers also like to have students use CSR with the local newspaper. In Lourdes Formoso's sixth-grade class, for example, each group selects a different story, implements CSR, and then shares with the rest of the class what they learned.

Chunking Text

Once you have selected the reading material for your class, you'll need to decide how large of a chunk of text students should read before stopping to Click and Clunk and Get the Gist. Many textbook chapters are divided into sections that are about two or three paragraphs long, just

about the right length for CSR. When using a shorter reading selection, such as from a *Weekly Reader*, you may prefer to have your students stop after every paragraph. When deciding how much text students should read before stopping, you'll want to consider how much time you have available to implement CSR. When students stop to Click and Clunk and Get the Gist more often, they may acquire a more thorough understanding of the text, but it takes longer. When students only stop a few times during reading, they will finish the passage more quickly, but may not learn the material as well.

CSR Learning Logs

Learning Logs are journals that provide a means for students to keep track of learning "as it happens." Logs can be spiral-bound notebooks or journals made by folding paper in half and stapling it with a construction paper cover. A different Learning Log can be created for each social studies or science unit. These logs provide written documentation of learning, thus assuring the individual accountability that facilitates cooperative learning. Logs also become excellent study guides. We have created various templates for CSR Learning Logs. They can be found in the Materials section at the end of this chapter. Choose the type you like best.

How to Use CSR Learning Logs

While implementing the Preview strategy before reading, we recommend that students write down what they already know about the day's topic in their Learning Logs. About one and a half minutes seems to be sufficient time for this. After recording their entries, students select their favorite ideas to share with the rest of the group. Next, they write down what they predict they will learn from the day's reading selection, and share their ideas. During reading, students should write down their clunks (and the clunk's meaning when they have figured it out). Some teachers like to have their students record their gists, and other teachers do not. It saves time to only record the passage's key ideas during Wrap Up. After reading, students should record their questions and the most important ideas they have learned.

Benefits

Learning Logs have many benefits. They provide a way for all students to participate actively in their groups and reinforce usage of the strategies. We have found this to be very beneficial for low-achieving students, students with LD, and English language learners who may tune out during large class discussions. Students are told that the important thing is to record their ideas—they aren't graded on spelling or penmanship. This time to reflect about and record their ideas seems to help students gather their thoughts. Those who usually don't participate in whole class discussions develop confidence and feel prepared to share their ideas in small groups.

Another benefit of CSR Learning Logs is that they facilitate classroom management. When only one student in a group serves as the recorder and has the job of writing down the group's ideas, as with some cooperative learning structures, other students in the group tend to use this "down time" to drift off task. Because with CSR every student records his or her ideas, everyone stays on task. Many teachers have commented positively about the way Learning Logs keep all students on task.

Log entries become a permanent record of the learning that takes place in CSR groups. They provide the teacher with a way to check students' progress and understanding of key concepts. Teachers have shared with us that they particularly find it useful that students record their clunks and group-generated definitions. Teachers can quickly look at students' logs to determine if students accurately figured out the meanings of challenging words, or perhaps still have some misunderstandings that need to be rectified. Learning Logs also can become a form of portfolio assessment. We know special education teachers who have written Individualized

Educational Program (IEP) goals for their students with disabilities based on projected growth as demonstrated in CSR Learning Logs.

Logs also help students learn note-taking skills. They become excellent study guides for chapter or unit tests. Some teachers have their students take their logs home and study them as homework. Finally, logs can serve as a springboard for follow-up activities (see the section on follow-up activities in the previous chapter).

CSR Cue Cards and Sheets

Cue cards and cue sheets outline the procedures to be followed in cooperative learning groups and provide structure and support for students while they are learning CSR. Each cooperative learning group role comes with a corresponding cue card or sheet that explains the steps to be followed to fulfill that role. Cue cards and sheets help students stay focused and on task, and increase their confidence. We have found that, with cue cards, even students with LD, low-achieving students, and English language learners can successfully be group leaders.

We have created different cue cards and sheets for different grade levels (see Materials section for samples). Cues are presented on cards so that they can also be used as bookmarks or placeholders while reading. Select the version that you prefer.

Many teachers discontinue use of the cue cards when their students feel secure in carrying out their roles. After all, an important purpose of CSR is to encourage students to engage in meaningful discussions about text content. When students rely on cue cards extensively, their dialogue is in jeopardy of becoming too rote or stilted. Students may find discarding cue cards difficult to do as they enjoy the comfort and confidence that these cards provide even after they are highly familiar with the strategy.

Teachers have adapted CSR Cue Cards in various ways over the years. At one school, the teachers separated the prompts on every cue card and wrote each prompt on a different 2" by 3" card. These cards were then hole-punched in the upper right hand corner and assembled on rings. Each set was a different color and corresponded with a different role. Students flipped through their cards as they carried out their roles. Teachers at the school shared with us that they felt this adaptation made CSR more "game-like." We have seen other teachers write the prompts for each role in large letters on posters that they hung on a bulletin board or hung from rolling chart holders that were brought out into the center of the room when it was time for CSR.

CSR Clunk Cards

Clunk Cards can be used by the Clunk Expert to assist the group in figuring out difficult words. Each Clunk Card contains a different fix-up strategy. The Clunk Expert first asks the group if anyone already knows the meaning of a classmate's clunk. If no one does, he or she then reads these cards one at a time and directs the other students in the group to follow the instructions until someone comes up with an accurate definition. To help students develop proficiency using the Clunk Cards, many teachers provide their students with extra practice figuring out challenging vocabulary words. They do this by putting sentences or short paragraphs up on the overhead projector, each with a difficult word. Then students in their cooperative learning groups are directed to: (a) figure out the meaning of the target word, and (b) identify the fix-up strategy that is most useful for this purpose. Sample Clunk Cards can be found in the Materials section at the end of this chapter.

Timer

Timers are optional. Some teachers prefer to maintain the role of timekeeper rather than turning this responsibility over to their students, particularly in the third and fourth grades. Other teachers like to provide each group with a timer and have one student in every group serve as the timekeeper. Kitchen timers work well for this purpose. Timers that can be set digitally for an exact time are best. Students can easily set these by themselves. Timers can help groups remain on task and not get excessively bogged down with any one strategy or step in the Collaborative Strategic Reading process. For example, the timekeeper might say, "We have one and a half minutes to write down everything we already know about the topic." Then the timekeeper would set the timer for 90 seconds (see the Timekeeper's Cue Card for more information).

An alternative is for the teacher to set one timer and direct students in their groups to carry out the strategies for a set period of time. We recommend using this procedure for the first few days that students work together in cooperative groups so that they can develop an understanding of how the process works. Yet, once groups can function more autonomously, they should be encouraged to do so.

Score Cards

Score Cards are another optional item. If you would like your class to earn points, then one student in each group should be assigned the role of scorekeeper. The scorekeeper follows a Cue Card to find out when to award points, and records these points on a Score Card. Points can be an excellent way to help motivate students to stay on task, to encourage students to participate, to progress quickly, and to cooperate with one another. Students seem to enjoy earning points and adding them up just to see which group has earned the most and deserves "a special round of applause." Points add an extra element of fun to CSR and appeal to teachers who like "game-like" activities. However, we have seen classes where students seemed to be paying too much attention to earning points rather than what they were learning. If you would like scorekeeping to be a part of CSR in your class, it is important that earning points doesn't become a distraction. The primary goal of CSR is to facilitate content area learning. A sample score card can be found in the Materials section at the end of this chapter.

Overhead Transparencies

We find it very helpful to use overhead transparencies when teaching the CSR strategies and roles to students. In addition to the sample masters included here, you might also wish to make the Learning Logs and Cue Sheets into transparencies. Samples are available at the end of this chapter.

Sample Materials

CSR Learning Log

Name _____ Date _____

Topic _____

Preview

Brainstorm: What I already know about the topic.

Predict: What I might learn about the topic.

Clunks

Get the Gist

* Name the who or what.

* Say it in ten words or less.

* Tell the most important information.

Wrap Up

Questions.

What I learned.

CSR Learning Log

Today's Topic _____ Date _____

Before Reading	After Reading
Preview	**Wrap Up**
What I already know about the topic.	Questions about the important ideas in the passage.
What I predict I will learn.	What I learned.

During Reading   Clunks

CSR Learning Log

Today's Topic _____

Date _____

Before Reading **Preview**	During Reading **Clunks & Gists**	After Reading **Wrap Up**
What I already know about the topic.		Questions about the important ideas in the passage.
What I predict I will learn.		What I learned.

CSR Learning Log

Today's Topic _____   Date _____

Before Reading	Preview 👁	What I already know about the topic. What I think I will learn.
During Reading	Clunks & Gists 🔍	1st section of the passage. 2nd section of the passage. 3rd section of the passage.
After Reading	Wrap Up ✦	Questions about the important ideas in the passage. What I learned.

CSR Leader's Cue Cards

Before Reading	During Reading	After Reading
Preview	**Read**	**Wrap Up**

Before Reading

Preview

S: We know that today's topic is _____.

S: Let's brainstorm and write everything we already know about the topic in our learning logs.

S: Who would like to share their best ideas?

S: Now let's predict. Look at the title, pictures, and headings and think about what we might learn today. Write your ideas in your Learning Logs.

S: Who would like to share their best ideas?

During Reading

Read

S: Who would like to read the next section?

Click and Clunk

S: Did everyone understand what we read? If you did not, write your clunks in your Learning Log.

[If someone has a clunk]

S: Clunk Expert, please help us out.

Get the Gist

S: It's time to Get the Gist. Gist Expert, please help us out.

Go back and do all of the steps in this column over for each section.

After Reading

Wrap Up

S: Now let's think of some questions to check if we really understood what we read. Remember to start your questions with who, when, what, where, why, or how. Everyone write your questions in your Learning Log.

S: Who would like to share their best question?

S: In our Learning Logs, let's write down as much as we can about what we learned.

S: Let's go around the group and each share something we learned.

Compliments and Suggestions

S: The Encourager has been watching carefully and will now tell us two things we did really well as a group today.

S: Is there anything that would help us do even better next time?

CSR Cue Cards

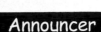

Announcer

Remember to make sure only one person talks at a time!

Preview

* Call on at least two people to say what they know.
* Call on at least two people to say what they think they will learn.

Read

* Call on different people to read.

Clunks

* Call on students who have clunks.
* Call on students to help fix clunks.

Get the Gist

* Call on one person to say the gist.
* Call on at least one other person to say his or her version of the gist.

Wrap Up

* Call on two students to share their best questions.
* Call on students to answer the questions.
* Call on all students to say something they learned.

Timekeeper

Preview

* We have 1 minute and 30 seconds to write what we know.
* We have 1 minute and 30 seconds to write what we think we will learn.

Read, Click and Clunk, Get the Gist

* Before the group begins reading each section way, "We have 6 minutes for this section."

Wrap Up

* Before wrap up begins say, "We have 5 minutes to wrap up."
* We have 2 minutes to write our questions.
* We have 1 minute to write what we learned.

CSR Cue Cards

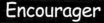

Encourager

Remember, you are responsible for telling your classmates when they do a good job!

Preview

Brainstorm:
* Tell someone they did a good job saying what they already know.

Predict:
* Tell someone they did a good job saying what they think they will learn.

Click and Clunk

* Tell someone they did a good job figuring out a clunk.

Get the Gist

* Tell someone they did a good job getting the gist.

Wrap Up

Ask Questions:
* Tell someone they asked a good question.

Review:
* Tell someone they did a good job saying what they learned.

Compliments and Suggestions

* Tell two things your group did well today.
* Tell two things your group can do even better next time.

Scorekeeper

Preview

* Give 1 point each time someone tells what they already know and predicts what the group will learn.

Click and Clunk

* Give 3 points if your group worked together to figure out the clunks or if you all understood everything you read.

Get the Gist

* Give 1 point for everyone who says their own version of the gist.
* Give 4 points if you finish the entire section in 6 minutes or less.

Wrap Up

* Give 1 point for each question generated.
* Give 1 point for each question answered.
* Give 1 extra point for each really good "why" or "how" question.
* Give 5 points if everyone cooperated and helped each other.

CSR Cue Cards

Clunk Expert's Cue Card

Ask: What is your clunk?

Ask: Does anyone know the meaning of the clunk?

If YES:

* *Say:* Please explain what the clunk means.

* *Ask:* Does everyone understand now? *Check for understanding.*

If NO:

1. *Say:* Reread the sentence with the clunk and look for key ideas to help you figure out the word. Think about what makes sense.

   Can anyone now explain the meaning of the clunk? *If no, go to Step 2.*

2. *Say:* Reread the sentences before and after the sentence with the clunk looking for clues.

   Can anyone now explain the meaning of the clunk? *If no, go to Step 3.*

3. *Say:* Look for a prefix or suffix in the word that might help.

   Can anyone now explain the meaning of the clunk? *If no, go to Step 4.*

4. *Say:* Break the word apart and look for smaller words you know.

   Can anyone now explain the meaning of the clunk? *If no, go to Step 5.*

5. *Ask the teacher for help.*

Gist Expert's Cue Card

1. What is the most important idea we have learned about the topic so far? Everyone think of the gist and write it in your Learning Log.

2. Announcer, please call on someone to share their gist.

3. Does anyone have a different gist they would like to share?

4. Announcer, call on someone else to share their gist.

5. Help your group come up with a gist that includes the most important information, leaves out details, and is ten words or less.

CSR Leader's Cue Sheet

Before Reading

Preview

Brainstorm:

1. We know that today's topic is _____. We are going to brainstorm what we already know about this topic. We have _____ minutes for this activity. Timekeeper, start the timer.

2. Who would like to share their best ideas? We will earn one point for everyone who shares an idea. We have _____ minutes for this activity. Timekeeper, start the timer. Announcer, please call on someone with their hand raised.

(Continue until sharing is finished or time is up.)

Predict:

3. We are going to predict what we might learn today. We have _____ minutes for this activity. Timekeeper, start the timer.

4. It's time to share our best ideas. We will earn one point for everyone who shares an idea. We have _____ minutes for this activity. Timekeeper, start the timer. Who would like to share their best ideas? Announcer, please call on someone with their hand raised.

(Continue until sharing is finished or time is up.)

During Reading

Read

5. It's time to read, locate clunks, and get the gist of today's reading. We will earn two points for every clunk we figure out together. We will earn one point for everyone who shares a gist. We have _____ minutes for this activity. Timekeeper, start the timer.

6. Who would like to read the section? Announcer, please call on someone with their hand raised.

Click and Clunk

7. It's time to figure out our clunks. Look through the section we just read. Write your clunks in your Learning Log.

8. Does anyone have any clunks?
   ○ Yes — Clunk expert, please help us out. ○ No — (Go to Get the Gist)

Get the Gist

9. It's time to Get the Gist. Gist Expert, please help us out.

Go back to 6 and do all of the steps on this page for each section that the group reads.

Collaborative Strategic Reading | **89**

CSR Leader's Cue Sheet (continued)

Wrap Up

Answering Questions:

10. It is time to ask and answer questions. We will earn one point for everyone who asks a question and one point for everyone who answers a question. We will have _____ minutes for this activity. Timekeeper, start the timer. Who would like to share their best question? Announcer, please call on someone with their hand raised. Who would like to answer the question? Announcer, please call on someone with their hand raised.

    (Continue until sharing is finished or time is up.)

Reviewing:

11. It's time to review. We will have _____ minutes to write what we learned. Timekeeper, start the timer.
12. Let's go around the group and each share something we learned. We will earn one point for everyone who shares something they learned. We will have _____ minutes for this activity. Timekeeper, start the timer. Announcer, please call on people.

Compliments and Suggestions

13. The Encourager has been watching carefully and will tell us one or two things we did really well as a group.
14. Is there anything that would help us do even better next time?

CSR Clunk Expert's Cue Sheet

1. What is your clunk?

2. Does anyone know the meaning of the clunk?

   ○ **YES**

   * Announcer, please call on someone with their hand raised.
   * Ask them to explain how they figured out the clunk.
   * Everyone, write the meaning in your Learning Log.

   ○ **NO**

   If NO, follow these steps until you know the meaning of the clunk and are ready to write it in your Learning Log.

   STEP 1: Read the sentence with the clunk and look for key ideas to help you figure out the word. Think about what makes sense.

   Raise your hand if you can explain the meaning of the clunk. (If NO, go to STEP 2.)

   STEP 2: Reread the sentence with the clunk and the sentences before and after the clunk looking for clues.

   Raise your hand if you can explain the meaning of the clunk. (If NO, go to STEP 3.)

   STEP 3: Look for a prefix or suffix in the word that might help.

   Raise your hand if you can explain the meaning of the clunk. (If NO, go to STEP 4.)

   STEP 4: Break the word apart and look for smaller words that you know.

   Raise your hand if you can explain the meaning of the clunk. (If NO, go to STEP 5.)

   STEP 5: Ask the teacher for help.

CSR Gist Expert's Cue Sheet

1. What is the most important idea we have learned about the topic so far? Everyone think of the gist and write it in your Learning Log.

2. Announcer, please call on someone to share their gist.

3. Does anyone have a different gist they would like to share?

4. Announcer, call on someone else to share their gist.

5. Help your group come up with a gist that includes the most important information, leaves out details, and is ten words or less.

CSR Encourager's Cue Sheet

During CSR

* When people in your group say a really good answer, compliment them.
* When people in your group don't seem to be participating, encourage them.

After CSR

A. When your group works well, what does that look like and what does it sound like? Say one thing about how the group cooperated and one thing about what helped the group learn.

Here are some ideas that will help you.

Cooperation:
1. Everyone in the group kept their voices low.
2. We treated each other with respect.
3. The group was really organized.
4. Everyone did their job well.
5. We cooperated with each other.
6. Everyone participated.
7. We managed our time well.
8. We took turns speaking.
9. Everyone was involved.

Learning:
1. The group tried their best.
2. The group figured out the clunks really well.
3. The group came up with good gists.
4. We learned a lot today.
5. The group's discussions were good.
6. We asked many thinking questions.
7. We asked many different kinds of questions.
8. Most of our answers were correct.
9. The group put a lot of thought into the questions that were asked.

B. Is there anything that would help us do better?

Here are some ideas that will help you.
1. We need to cooperate a little better.
2. Everyone should be involved.
3. We were a little noisy.
4. Remember to raise your hand.
5. Remember not to interrupt while others are speaking.
6. We need to be a little more organized.
7. We need to use our time better.

Click and Clunk Practice Sentences

Practice figuring out these clunks. What fix-up strategies did you use?

1. Everyday Michele runs, rides her bike, and swims. She hopes that some day she can be a <u>triathlete</u> in the Olympics.

   What does <u>triathlete</u> mean?

2. During the summer birds <u>molt</u>, or lose their feathers.

   What does <u>molt</u> mean?

3. The speaker did not pay any attention to the <u>heckler</u> who kept yelling rude comments from the back of the room.

   What does <u>heckler</u> mean?

4. A snake's body can bend and twist easily. It is very <u>supple</u>. It can move smoothly around sharp corners and slip through narrow places.

   What does <u>supple</u> mean?

5. Some bats have long, <u>thin</u> <u>snouts</u> that fix deep into flowers to sip nectar.

   What does <u>snout</u> mean?

6. The rat <u>hightailed</u> out of there as fast as he could.

   What does <u>hightailed</u> mean?

7. You will meet friends who will share your favorite <u>pastimes</u>.

   What does <u>pastimes</u> mean?

8. The United States <u>exports</u> more goods to China now that the two countries have reached a trade agreement.

   What does <u>exports</u> mean?

9. Rhythmic gymnastics was dropped from the Olympics in 1956 and <u>reinstated</u> in 1984.

   What does <u>reinstated</u> mean?

Bonus Question

10. The peace talks had come to a <u>standstill</u>. Neither side would <u>compromise</u>, or give in. Finally there was a <u>breakthrough</u> in the <u>negotiations</u> when the two sides agreed to a <u>cease-fire</u>. They promised to stop fighting for one month while their talks continued.

    What do <u>standstill</u>, <u>compromise</u>, <u>breakthrough</u>, <u>negotiations</u>, and <u>cease-fire</u> mean?

Adapted from the Reciprocal Teaching Staff Development Manual by Palincsar, David, & Brown.

Sample Clunk Cards

CLUNK CARD #1

Reread the sentence with the clunk and look for key ideas to help you figure out the word. Think about what makes sense.

CLUNK CARD #2

Reread the sentences before and after the clunk looking for clues.

CLUNK CARD #3

Look for a prefix or suffix in the word that might help.

CLUNK CARD #4

Break the word apart and look for smaller words that you know.

Sample Score Card

1	2	3	4	5	6	7	8	9	10	11	12	13	14	15
16	17	18	19	20	21	22	23	24	25	26	27	28	29	30
31	32	33	34	35	36	37	38	39	40	41	42	43	44	45
46	47	48	49	50	51	52	53	54	55	56	57	58	59	60
61	62	63	64	65	66	67	68	69	70	71	72	73	74	75
76	77	78	79	80	81	82	83	84	85	86	87	88	89	90
91	92	93	94	95	96	97	98	99	100	101	102	103	104	105
106	107	108	109	110	111	112	113	114	115	116	117	118	119	120
121	122	123	124	125	126	127	128	129	130	131	132	133	134	135
136	137	138	139	140	141	142	143	144	145	146	147	148	149	150
151	152	153	154	155	156	157	158	159	160	161	162	163	164	165
166	167	168	169	170	171	172	173	174	175	176	177	178	179	180
181	182	183	184	185	186	187	188	189	190	191	192	193	194	195
196	197	198	199	200	201	202	203	204	205	206	207	208	209	210
211	212	213	214	215	216	217	218	219	220	221	222	223	224	225
226	227	228	229	230	231	232	233	234	235	236	237	238	239	240
241	242	243	244	245	246	247	248	249	250	251	252	253	254	255
256	257	258	259	260	261	262	263	264	265	266	267	268	269	270
271	272	273	274	275	276	277	278	279	280	281	282	283	284	285
286	287	288	289	290	291	292	293	294	295	296	297	298	299	300
301	302	303	304	305	306	307	308	309	310	311	312	313	314	315
316	317	318	319	320	321	322	323	324	325	326	327	328	329	330
331	332	333	334	335	336	337	338	339	340	341	342	343	344	345
346	347	348	349	350	351	352	353	354	355	356	357	358	359	360
361	362	363	364	365	366	367	368	369	370	371	372	373	374	375
376	377	378	379	380	381	382	383	384	385	386	387	388	389	390
391	392	393	394	395	396	397	398	399	400	401	402	403	404	405
406	407	408	409	410	411	412	413	414	415	416	417	418	419	420
421	422	423	424	425	426	427	428	429	430	431	432	433	434	435
436	437	438	439	440	441	442	443	444	445	446	447	448	449	450
451	452	453	454	455	456	457	458	459	460	461	462	463	464	465
466	467	468	469	470	471	472	473	474	475	476	477	478	479	480
481	482	483	484	485	486	487	488	489	490	491	492	493	494	495
496	497	498	499	500										

Overhead Transparency Masters

Preview

Preview before reading. When you Preview, look at the title, subheadings, pictures, and skim the text to look for key words.

Preview has two steps:

STEP 1: Brainstorm

✴ Think about what you already know about the topic.

✴ Write it in your Learning Log.

STEP 2: Predict

✴ Think about what you might learn.

✴ Write your ideas in the Learning Log.

Click and Clunk

Clicks:

When you understand what you read, everything "clicks" along smoothly.

Clunks:

When you don't understand what you read, "clunk," you stop. When you get to a clunk, use the fix-up strategies to try and figure out what the clunk means.

Clunk Fix-Up Strategies

1. Reread the sentence with the clunk and look for key ideas to help you figure out the word. Think about what makes sense.

2. Reread the sentences before and after the clunk, looking for clues.

3. Look for a prefix or suffix in the word that might help.

4. Break the word apart and look for smaller words that you know.

Collaborative Strategic Reading

Get the Gist

1. Name the "who" (person) or "what" (place or thing) the paragraph or section was mostly about.

2. What is the most important information about the who or what?

3. Write the gist in ten words or less.

Wrap Up

Wrap Up after finishing the reading assignment. Wrap Up has two steps:

STEP 1: Questioning

* Think of questions and write them in your Learning Log.

* Ask and answer questions.

STEP 2: Review

* Think about the important information you learned from the reading.

* Write the important information in your Learning Log.

* State something important you have learned.

Sample Question Stems

1. Why do you think _____?

2. How were _____ and _____ alike?

3. How were _____ and _____ different?

4. What do you think would happen if _____?

5. What do you think caused _____ to happen?

6. What other solution can you think of for the problem?

7. What might have prevented the problem of _____ from happening?

8. What are the strengths (or weaknesses) of _____?

Question Types

1. **Right There**

   The answer is easy to find in the reading. The words used to make up the question and the words used to answer the question are **right there** in the same sentence.

2. **Think and Search**

   The answer to the question is in the reading. The answer is made up of information that comes from more than one sentence or paragraph. You have to put together information from different parts of the reading to find the answer.

3. **The Author and You**

   The answer to the question is not in the reading. Think about what the author tells you and what you already know.

Time Allotments

Before Reading

Preview

Brainstorm:

   1. Write: _____ minutes

   2. Share: _____ minutes

Predict:

   3. Write: _____ minutes

   4. Share: _____ minutes

During Reading

   5. Read, Click and Clunk, & Get the Gist: _____ minutes

After Reading

Wrap Up

   6. Write questions: _____ minutes

   7. Answer questions: _____ minutes

   8. Write what you learned: _____ minutes

   9. Share: _____ minutes

CSR Learning Log

Today's Topic _____ Date _____

Before Reading	After Reading
Preview What I already know about the topic. What I predict I will learn.	**Wrap Up** Questions about the important ideas in the passage. What I learned.

During Reading — Clunks

Collaborative Strategic Reading

CSR's Plan for Strategic Reading

Before Reading

Preview

1. BRAINSTORM — What do we already know about the topic?

2. PREDICT — What do we predict we will learn about the topic when we read the passage?

During Reading

Click and Clunk

1. Were there any parts that were hard to understand (clunks)?

2. How can we fix the clunks? Use fix-up strategies:
   (a) Reread the sentence with the clunk and look for key ideas to help you understand.
   (b) Reread the sentences before and after the clunk to look for clues.
   (c) Look for a prefix or suffix in the word.
   (d) Break the word apart and look for smaller words.

Get the Gist

1. What is the most important person, place, or thing in this section?

2. What is the most important idea about the person, place, or thing?

After Reading

Wrap Up

1. ASK QUESTIONS — What questions check whether we understand the most important information in the passage? Can we answer the questions?

2. REVIEW — What did we learn?

Adaptations to CSR for Secondary Students

Mrs. Penney, a seventh grade general education science teacher, was concerned that a significant number of students in her classes were reading below grade level and had difficulty comprehending content presented in the labs and science textbook. These students included both low achievers and students with reading disabilities. In particular, these students demonstrated limited background information for content area concepts, possessed below average vocabulary skills, and did not appear to use comprehension strategies to monitor their reading. Additionally, these students typically did not fare well on the district's high stakes assessment, as they seemed to struggle with comprehension skills such as identifying the main idea, summarizing, and drawing inferences. Mrs. Penney was concerned about the apparent lack of interest and motivation demonstrated by the students to read the text and participate in small group discussions. Although Mrs. Penney was responsible for teaching the science curriculum as designated by the school district, she sensed an urgency in teaching her struggling students comprehension strategies to help them become more independent, successful readers. Consequently, Mrs. Penney talked with the

Chapter at a Glance

- **Glimpse From the Classroom**
- **Teaming**
- **What Instructional Materials are Useful for CSR?**
- **What are Grouping Options for CSR?**
- **What are Scheduling Considerations for Using CSR?**
- **How is Content Area Vocabulary Taught With CSR?**
- **How is CSR Integrated Into Content Area Instruction?**

other content area teachers on her team, including the special education teacher, to work collaboratively on comprehension strategies to help their struggling students tackle text.

Mrs. Penney's experiences with struggling readers are not uncommon because, as students progress through the upper-elementary and secondary level grades (middle and high school), academic instruction in content area curriculum such as English language arts, social studies, and science shifts from an emphasis on *"learning how to read"* to *"using reading to learn."* For many students, this shift in learning is challenging because they do not possess the necessary requisite skills to read content material successfully. Content area reading instruction integrates reading and language arts skills within all disciplines; this implies that all teachers are responsible for helping students use reading and language arts skills to learn the content of the subject area that they teach.

The ability to comprehend text is crucial because of the large amounts of information students must take in (Rivera & Smith, 1997), the vocabulary they must learn (West, 1978), and the text structures (i.e., cueing systems that refer to how ideas are interrelated to convey meaning such as comparison, sequencing, and cause-and-effect relationships) that are used to organize this material (Meyer & Rice, 1984). In content area reading, students interact with text to interpret and construct meaning before, during, and after reading by using their prior knowledge and basic reading skills, such as word identification strategies (e.g., structural analysis, syllabication) to decode unfamiliar words and context clues to figure out the meaning of vocabulary (Lenz & Hughes, 1990).

For secondary students who struggle with reading, content area reading can be overwhelmingly difficult because they typically lack the basic reading strategies and skills needed to succeed in textbook-based instruction as compared to their typically achieving peers (see **Table 5-1**).

Most students who struggle with reading, including students who have reading disabilities, need assistance to integrate the new content information with their prior knowledge and to comprehend what they have read. In this chapter, we take what you have learned about CSR in earlier chapters in this book and provide adaptations for using CSR at the secondary level to accommodate the learning needs of struggling students. Although the implementation of the four strategies (Preview, Click and Clunk, Get the Gist, and Wrap Up) remains intact, our experiences working with secondary teachers have taught us that, because of the nature of content area instruction (textbooks and vocabulary demands) and the reading needs of struggling students, adaptations to CSR are necessary. The adaptations to CSR that we offer include teaming, instructional materials, grouping arrangements, scheduling, vocabulary instruction, and integration of CSR into content area instruction.

Teaming

When working with secondary level teachers, we have found the middle school teaming concept to be helpful in teaching and implementing CSR. In this model, a grade level might have two or three teams depending on the number of students. A team usually consists of the English language arts, science, social studies, math, special education teachers, and a teaching assistant, if one is assigned to the team. The teaming model consists of two major components that are conducive to CSR instruction. First, typically, the team has the same planning time, which permits discussion about how instruction will be delivered, issues pertaining to certain students, and so forth. Second, because the implementation of CSR involves teaching the students the strategies and then having them apply the strategies to content text, the team decides who will take the lead in teaching the

Table 5-1

Characteristics of Good and Poor Readers

Good Readers

Before Reading

* Consider what they already know about the topic

* Use text features (e.g., boldface, headings, illustrations) to get a sense of what they will read

During Reading

* Monitor their reading by recognizing comprehension problems and using "fix-up" strategies

* Use context clues to figure out the meaning of vocabulary and concepts

* Identify the main idea and important details

* Read fluently

* Use word identification strategies to decode unfamiliar words

* Recognize and use text structures to gain meaning from reading

After Reading

* Summarize reading

* Reflect on content

* Draw inferences

Poor Readers

Before Reading

* Begin reading without a purpose

* Do not consider their background knowledge about the topic

* Lack motivation or interest

During Reading

* Move through the text, even if they do not understand what they have read

* Do not read fluently

* Do not recognize text structures

* Lack strategies to figure out new words

* Lack strategies to repair comprehension problems

After Reading

* Cannot summarize important points

* Do not use strategies to reflect on reading

Taken from Bryant, D. P., N. Ugel, S. Thompson, & A. Hamff. (1999). Strategies to promote content area reading instruction. *Intervention in School and Clinic, 34*(5), 293–302. Austin, TX: PRO-ED.

strategies. For instance, the English language arts teacher might volunteer to teach "fix-up strategies" and "Get the Gist" because these two approaches fit naturally within the English language arts curricular domain. The teacher might provide practice using these strategies with easier than normal text so that the students are learning the strategies and are not bogged down by grade level reading material, which might be challenging for struggling readers.

Science and social studies teachers might volunteer to teach "Preview" and "Wrap Up" because these two strategies fit well with expository text material found in these content area classes. Once the students have been introduced to the strategies, all teachers make a commitment to implementing CSR at least twice a week. All classes should prominently display the fix-up strategies on a poster.

Although there is less text reading in math than in the other classes, math vocabulary can be challenging. The students might use the clunk card that tells students to break words apart or some other vocabulary strategy (see the vocabulary section below). Certainly, "Preview" and "Wrap Up" can be used in math as well.

The special education teacher plays a critical role in the implementation of CSR. For example, she might take aside a homogeneous group of students who require additional instruction on one or more of the strategies. Alternatively, the special education teacher might work with a heterogeneous group, including students with disabilities, on a reading assignment to problem solve the use of fix-up strategies, to find the gist, and to generate good Wrap Up questions. He or she also can ensure that IEP identified adaptations are in place as students work through the CSR process. The team's commitment to implementing CSR for portions of time during the week demonstrates to students that these strategies are applicable across content areas. As one sixth-grade student said, "I decided to learn the strategies because I realized I just couldn't get away from them."

What Instructional Materials are Useful for CSR?

Secondary teachers report that their students benefit from a variety of instructional materials written at different grade levels. Particularly, secondary-age students who are struggling readers enjoy materials that feature articles about topics they are studying in their content classes but that are written at a lower reading level. Teachers have reported that supplemental materials for content instruction should contain age-appropriate material designed to motivate students to read and to decrease their reading-related frustration. It should also be linked in some way to the curriculum being taught.

A list of publishers who offer high interest/ controlled vocabulary reading materials is shown in **Table 5-2**. Reading materials can be selected for both expository and narrative text structures and for use in supplementing classroom instruction.

In CSR, teachers are encouraged to select materials that contain **physical text features**, such as boldface terms, charts and illustrations, and headings, especially for expository text. These physical features help students develop a sense of the chapter's content and facilitate the Preview step. Additional text features, such as objectives, discussion questions, chapter review questions, glossaries, and headings and subheadings also provide extra cues about the topic. Teachers report that using photos or videos to supplement instruction helps to activate prior knowledge and promote comprehension. Photos that contain illustrations of thematic topics or narrative settings work particularly well. For example, when teaching *To Kill a Mockingbird* the teacher can use black and white photos that depict depression era scenes to introduce the setting and period in which the novel takes place. Additionally, the teacher can use clips from the movie to illustration characterization.

Table 5-2

High Interest/Controlled Vocabulary Materials

Publishing Companies/Books

Academic Communication Associates
(888) 758–9558
  Narrative: classics

Capstone Press (888) 574–6711
  Narrative: classics, adventures, mysteries
  Expository: family, communities, native
    peoples, states, wildlife

Carson-Dellosa (800) 321–0943
  Narrative: adventures, mysteries
  Expository: biographies

Curriculum Associates (800) 225–0248
  Expository: nature, animals, sports

Educational Design (800) 221–9372
  Narrative: action
  Expository: biographies, multicultural,
    world events

Educators Publishing Service
(800) 435–7728
  Narrative: sports
  Expository: multicultural, world events,
    history

Globe Fearon (800) 872–8893
  Narrative: classics, action, science fiction,
    suspense, adventures, mysteries
  Expository: biographies, multicultural,
    world events, family, communities

High Noon Books (800) 422–7249
  Narrative: classics, adventures, mysteries,
    athletes
  Expository: natural disasters, biographies

Incentives for Learning (888) 238–2379
  Narrative: personal challenges, thrillers,
    adventures, mysteries, athletes, classics
  Expository: holidays, biographies

New Readers Press (800) 448–8878
  Expository: heroes, bibliographies,
    friendships

News for You (800) 448–8878
  Narrative: national and international
    articles and essays
  Expository: national and international
    news

PCI Educational Publishing
(800) 594–4263
  Narrative: adventures, mysteries, classics,
    short stories
  Expository: heroes, escapes, disasters,
    body science

Phoenix Learning Resources
(800) 221–1274
  Narrative: classics, art, poetry
  Expository: life science, earth science,
    physical science

Steck-Vaughn (800) 531–5015
  Narrative: classics
  Expository: geography, challenges,
    adventures, rescues

Sundance (800) 343–8204
  Narrative: classics, adventure,
    science fiction, thrillers
  Expository: ships, animal attacks,
    biographies

Publishing Companies/Magazines

National Geographic (800) 638–4077

National Wildlife Federation
(800) 611–1599

Smithsonian Institute (800) 827–0227

Graphic organizers can be used to organize vocabulary words (see the Semantic Map in the vocabulary section), to depict characterization, and to illustrate content using text structure formats. For example, as seen in **Figure 5-1**, students can use the rich language of the novel to depict the character's attributes.

What are Grouping Options for CSR?

CSR is often taught using small groups of students, three to five students in a group. Cooperative learning practices employed in these small groups seem to help students of differing abilities tackle text. Science teachers who use small groups for lab exercises have expressed comfort with this grouping option. However, not all secondary level teachers use small groups for instructional purposes. Whole class instruction tends to be the norm. We suggest, however, that teachers at least combine students working in pairs with whole class work.

Teachers can begin the lesson, then ask students to work in pairs to complete the "Preview" step. Students can report their ideas to the large group. We strongly recommend that students work in pairs during the "Click and Clunk" and "Get the Gist" steps; that is, students should take turns reading the paragraphs or passages during CSR. Regardless of the grouping format, each student should complete his or her own Learning Log.

Eventually, once teachers are comfortable with students' abilities to work in pairs, small groups of three to four students can be considered. This grouping option will provide students the opportunity to implement cooperative learning roles, such as leader, clunk expert, and announcer.

Figure 5-1

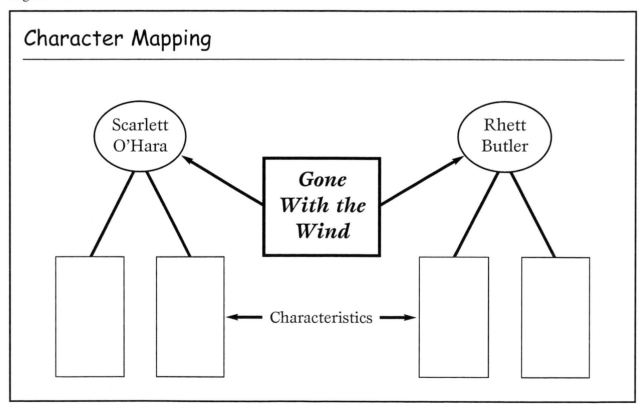

112 | *Collaborative Strategic Reading*

What are the Scheduling Considerations for Using CSR?

Secondary school schedules vary from school district to school district. For example, some districts have adopted the more traditional six to eight periods a day where each class period ranges from 45 to 60 minutes and students receive instruction in each subject area. Other school districts have moved to a "block scheduling" format. In this arrangement, class periods usually last for 90 minutes, but can run for as long as 120 minutes, and subjects are offered on alternating days.

Tips for Teachers

Mr. Johnson, a sixth grade social studies teacher with whom we have worked, offers these suggestions for using CSR within the context of secondary scheduling:

Secondary Scheduling
Timing is the Key: You Be the Judge

* 30 to 45 minutes of class time

* 2 to 3 times weekly

* once weekly for test/quiz preparation

How is Content Area Vocabulary Taught With CSR?

Content area vocabulary is considered an important component of CSR, particularly at the secondary level. Although "Click and Clunk" includes fix-up strategies for figuring out unknown words, concepts, phrases, and so forth, we have learned that, with secondary students, additional vocabulary instruction is often necessary.

Content Area Vocabulary Instruction

Vocabulary knowledge and reading comprehension are highly related. Each content area has its own language or vocabulary. Students who do not learn the meanings of a sufficient proportion of the new words will have difficulty understanding the assigned material. To comprehend their content area text, students must be able to determine the meanings of **general**, **specialized**, and **technical** vocabulary. **General vocabulary** consists of words students know and use as part of everyday activities. **Specialized vocabulary** consists of words that have specific meanings for content area subjects and have different meanings when used in other contexts. For example, the word "brush" has different meanings for art and geography teachers. **Technical vocabulary** includes words that relate specifically to each content area or topic. Students must learn the definitions of these words to understand content area text and to learn the language of the discipline.

We know that effective content area vocabulary instruction includes both explicit instruction in specific content-related words, concepts, and strategies that help students to learn words independently. Teachers model how to use context clues to determine the meanings of new words or concepts. This is part of the CSR "Click and Clunk" strategy. However, teachers must explicitly teach the meanings of a limited number of critical, technical vocabulary words prior to introducing a topic or a selection in each lesson. Finally, teachers help students link the new words to words they know and to their background knowledge, and provide students with multiple exposures to the word across contexts to help them develop a deeper understanding of its meaning. Thus, because of the extensive specialized and technical vocabulary for each content area, vocabulary strategies must be integrated into CSR instruction.

Content Area Vocabulary Strategies

Four vocabulary strategies are discussed here as ideas of techniques that can be used with CSR instruction, including Key Word Warm-Up, Semantic Mapping, Clunk Bug, and Word Map.

Key Word Warm-Up focuses on explicitly pre-teaching three to five key vocabulary words that students must understand to get started with the reading.

Tips for Teachers

Key Word Warm-Up

1. The teacher presents the words in one column along with their definitions in a second column on an overhead transparency.

2. The teacher calls on students to read the words and their definitions.

3. The teacher covers up the definition column, points to a word in the word column, and asks students to tell the definition of the word.

4. The teacher covers up the word column, points to a definition, and asks students to tell the word that matches the definition.

5. The teacher uses the words in sentences.

6. The teacher provides examples and non-examples; students say why or why not an example is good (e.g., "Tell me if this is an export. As part of the shoe industry, shoes are shipped to China to be sold.").

7. The teacher does a quick "rapid check:" says the word and the students say the definition.

As a part of "Preview" and throughout a lesson, Semantic Mapping can be used to help students conceptually organize their ideas about the topic to be read or ideas they have learned during the course of reading. The following "Tips for Teachers" provides an example of a lesson for using Semantic Mapping and **Figure 5-2** provides an example of a partially completed map.

Tips for Teachers

Semantic Map

1. The teacher identifies the concept to be taught.

2. The teacher models how to develop a semantic map.

3. The teacher writes the concept (the big idea) on the chalkboard or overhead transparency.

4. The teacher asks students to think of words (the little ideas) that are related to or associated with the concept.

5. The teacher writes these words and groups them into categories.

6. The teacher has students label each category.

7. Students work in pairs or small groups to construct a semantic map on a designated concept.

8. Students share their maps with the entire class.

9. The teacher concludes the session with a discussion of the concept, the related vocabulary words, categories, and the interrelationships among these words.

Evaluation

Students generate semantic maps that contain appropriate information for categories and subcategories. Students can explain in their own words the meaning of the concept and relate key vocabulary words.

Taken from *Enhancing Vocabulary Instruction for Secondary Students* (2000), Texas Center for Reading and Language Arts, College of Education, The University of Texas, Austin.

Figure 5-2

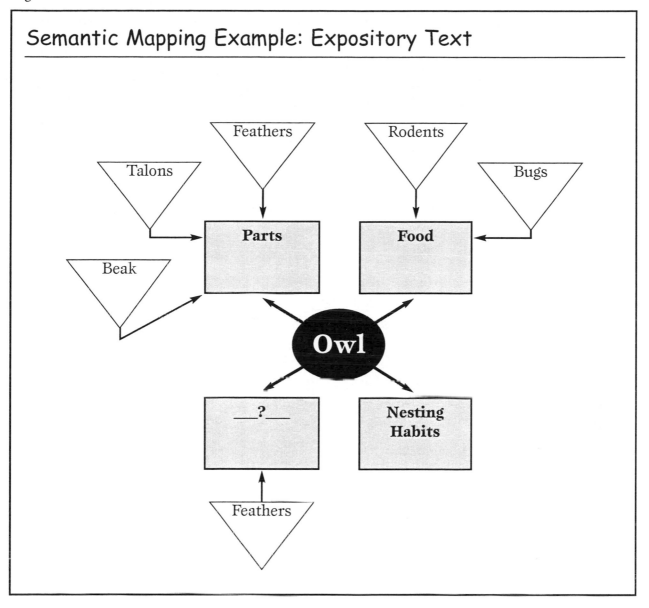

Semantic Mapping Example: Expository Text

Mr. Harry, a middle school science teacher, developed the Clunk Bug. Mr. Harry discovered that his students had difficulty not only with reading science text but also recognizing when the meanings of words were presented in context. Most of his students could not identify the signals for definitions commonly found in text (e.g., commas, dashes, bold or italicized print). For example, many of his students did not know that for the phrase, "haversack, a canvas shoulder bag that holds rations," the commas signaled the definition for haversack. Thus, Mr. Harry created the Clunk Bug where students placed the italicized word on the back of the bug and a key word from the definition on each leg. Students then wrote the definition of the word in their own words. Clunk Bugs adorned the wall during units of instruction. A sample Clunk Bug lesson and bug are shown in the following "Tips for Teachers" and **Figure 5-3**, respectively.

Clunk Bug

A. *Preparation*

1. Select several vocabulary words.

    ✳ Identify words that are defined in context using the "definition" type of context clue.

2. Prepare a list of signal words or punctuation.

    ✳ Select words or punctuation that indicate a vocabulary word is going to be defined in context.

    ✳ Signal words include: "is," "means," "i.e.," "that is."

    ✳ Signal punctuation includes: a dash, a comma.

B. *Instruction*

3. Have students read the sentence with the vocabulary word and write the vocabulary word on the back of the "Clunk Bug."

4. Have the students identify key words in the sentence and write one word on each of the Clunk Bug's legs.

5. Have the students use the words on the legs to write the definition of the vocabulary word.

6. Have students refer to the dictionary or the glossary in the textbook to verify their answers.

Evaluation

Using their own words, students write the definitions of the words.

Taken from *Enhancing Vocabulary Instruction for Secondary Students* (2000), Texas Center for Reading and Language Arts, College of Education, The University of Texas, Austin.

Finally, Word Map is a technique that can be used to provide instruction on the attributes of a word, examples and nonexamples of the word, and real life applications of the word. This technique causes students to think broadly about the word (examples, application) rather than focus exclusively on the definition. We have found that this technique can be used for vocabulary found in both narrative and expository text, and can be used to teach key vocabulary words prior to and during the lesson. The following "Tips for Teachers" provides a sample lesson for using the Word Map technique and **Figure 5-4** provides a template for students to complete.

Word Map

1. The teacher identifies key vocabulary words to be taught.

2. The teacher models how to generate a word map.

3. Students work in pairs to complete a word map on designated key vocabulary words.

4. Students share word maps with the entire class.

Evaluation

Students generate word maps that contain appropriate information for category, properties, examples, and real world applications. Students can state in their own words the meaning of the key vocabulary words.

Taken from *Enhancing Vocabulary Instruction for Secondary Students* (2000), Texas Center for Reading and Language Arts, College of Education, The University of Texas, Austin.

Figure 5-3

Clunk Bug Worksheet

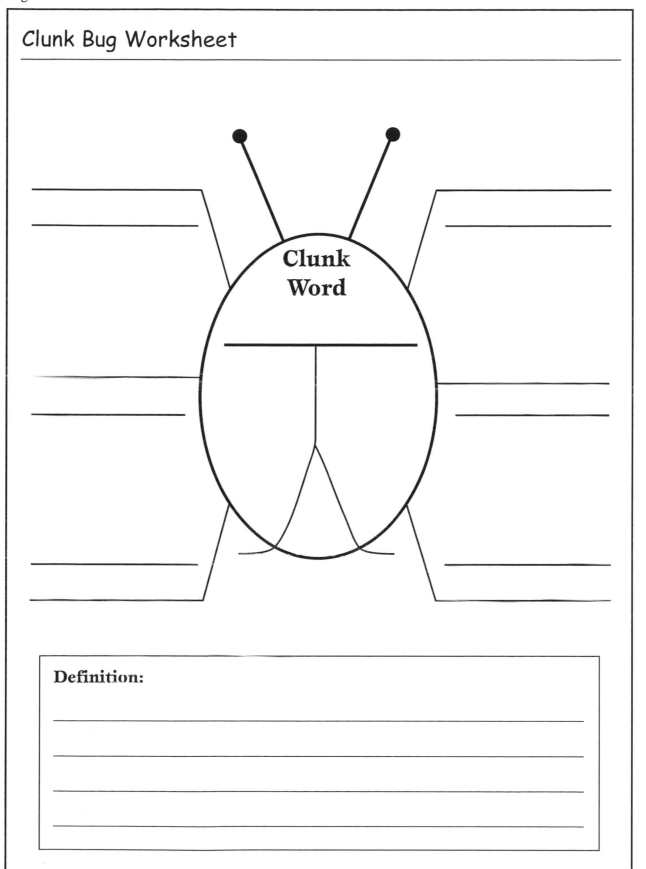

Definition:

Figure 5-4

Word Map Worksheet

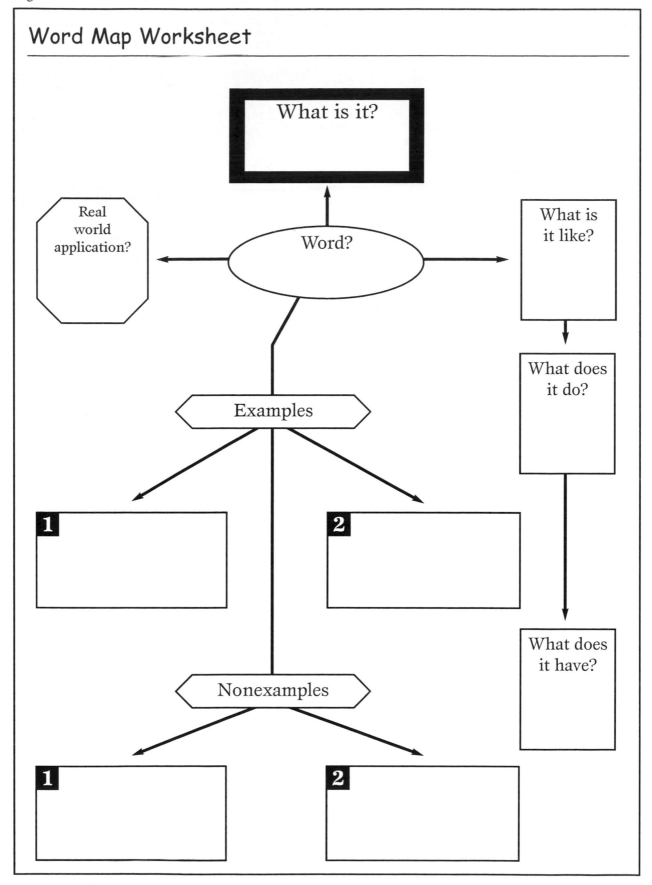

How is CSR Integrated Into Content Area Instruction?

CSR is a powerful set of reading comprehension strategies that helps students learn the curriculum. Teaching students to use these strategies can promote independent learning and provide struggling students with the tools they need to tackle content area text. We have learned in our work with secondary teachers, including general and special education teachers, that CSR can be integrated into literature-based instruction in English language arts classes and into instruction that focuses on social studies and science content.

As a first step, we recommend that teachers examine their curriculum for the semester and school year and then map out what they plan to teach during each block of time, such as a one-week social science unit, four weeks for a novel, and so forth. Next, we recommend that teachers map out how they will teach each instructional unit and how CSR can be integrated into the unit.

For example, in an English class, teachers might have students conduct research on the time setting for a novel before they read it. Class presentations and instruction might follow this research. Teachers might then want to examine the chapters and determine which sections will be taught using CSR and which sections will be taught using other instructional techniques. The same thinking can be applied to social studies or science units where teachers might want to integrate a variety of instructional techniques into lessons that include text reading and CSR. In the following paragraphs, we provide examples of how CSR can be integrated into instruction using both narrative and expository text.

Narrative

Narrative text structure focuses on **story grammar**, which includes characters, settings, themes, conflicts, plots, and conflict resolutions. This type of text structure is commonly found in elementary level reading material and in English language arts classes at the secondary level. Literature, and narrative text structure, lends itself to CSR; however, adaptations to the implementation process are necessary. Reciprocal Teaching (Palincsar & Brown, 1984) is better suited for narrative text. The following is an explanation of how CSR can be adapted and integrated into instruction based on our work with secondary level English language arts teachers. We use *To Kill a Mockingbird* as an example of how a novel can be taught with CSR. In this example, the teacher uses whole class instruction, student pairs, and literature circles as grouping arrangements.

Preparation

The teacher has mapped out six weeks of instruction on this novel. She collaborates with the social studies teacher and together they plan lessons that focus on the depression era and racial segregation. She begins with a vocabulary test.

Preview/Prior Knowledge/Vocabulary

To activate prior knowledge, the English teacher presents black and white photos of depression era scenes for small groups of students to discuss human conditions during that period. The teacher asks the students to generate questions they would ask the people in the photos. The teacher spends another lesson on introducing key vocabulary in the novel and especially in the first chapter by teaching the words explicitly (Key Word Warm-Up). In the next lesson, the teacher asks students to brainstorm what they know about the depression era and racial segregation and, using the Semantic Mapping technique, the students work in pairs to map their ideas. Students peruse the novel and note their predictions in their Learning Logs. The teacher asks student-pairs to share their maps and predictions. As the weeks progress, the teacher uses the prediction part of "Preview" prior to each chapter being read.

Click and Clunk/Get the Gist

Students are assigned to work in pairs to read the first four pages of the novel using the "Click and Clunk" and "Get the Gist" strategies during a timed 20-minute reading period. The lesson wraps up with the students sharing their clunks, which become part of their Learning Logs, and their gists. Students are asked to explain the fix-up strategies they used to figure out their clunks. The rest of the chapter is finished for homework. A follow-up activity is conducted during the next class period. As the novel unfolds, the teacher uses character mapping to help students identify the personal attributes of the main characters and Semantic Mapping to illustrate the important ideas related to the themes and literary elements in the novels. Clunks are added to the original Semantic Map to see how they fit with the organization of ideas, and vocabulary instruction and activities occur to teach new key words and to reinforce those that have been presented.

Wrap Up/Vocabulary

Each chapter concludes with the Wrap Up strategy where students generate a summary statement for the chapter's content and challenge questions, including who, what, when, where, why, how, and so forth. The summary statement and questions are recorded in the students' Learning Logs. Questions are often turned into a game format, such as Jeopardy, and students' questions can also appear on the chapter test. Sometimes, the teacher has students work in literature circles (small groups) and answer questions generated by another group of students.

Evaluation

Chapter tests along with vocabulary quizzes are given regularly so that information can be collected on the students' progress.

Expository

Expository text structures include enumeration, sequencing, comparison, cause-and-effect relationships, description, and problem-solution. Expository materials typically include physical text features such as headings and subheadings; chapter and section previews and summaries; and graphics, such as tables, charts, diagrams, figures, photographs, and illustrations. Expository text structure features are a good match with the CSR strategies; however, adaptations are suggested for struggling readers. The following is an explanation of how CSR can be adapted and integrated into social studies instruction; science teachers have found CSR to be useful when teaching their subject content as well. Cooperative learning is used to group students in this example.

Preparation

The social studies teacher will be teaching a unit on Greece and Greek Myths. The teacher has collaborated with the English language arts teacher so that students will be reading literature that complements the social studies unit. Supplemental materials have been selected to support the content in the textbook. Students have their own CSR folders, which contain their Learning Logs and supplemental reading material, and which are placed on their desks. Students' cooperative learning roles are assigned and everyone has a responsibility. A vocabulary test has been developed and the key learning points have been identified, which will be discussed with the review questions for the article. The teacher has designated two class periods to teach the entire lesson.

Introduction

The teacher begins by reminding students about their CSR roles (Leader, Clunk Expert, Gist Expert, Announcer, Encourager, Timekeeper) and discussing the goals of cooperative learning (individual accountability, group participation, social interaction). The teacher also briefly reviews the CSR strategies ("Preview," "Click and Clunk," "Get the Gist," and "Wrap Up").

Preview/Vocabulary

The teacher introduces the topic and provides explicit instruction on five key vocabulary words using the Key Word Warm-Up. The Word Map is another vocabulary strategy that is used to introduce key vocabulary. In cooperative learning groups, students brainstorm what they know about Greece and create Semantic Maps. They review the physical text features of the article and record their predictions in their Learning Logs. The teacher brings the class back together and asks each group to share their maps. She records their predictions on chart paper, which is posted for future reference.

Click and Clunk/Get the Gist/Vocabulary

The article contains five paragraphs about Greece and Greek mythology. The article explains that the myth was a favorite among the Greeks and that to the Greeks, Prometheus was a great hero. The article implies that to the Greeks the men in other countries were all barbarians and that the Greeks thought of themselves as very different from barbarians. The Greeks felt they were special. They felt like men who had been given the gift of Prometheus.

As the teacher walks around the class, she notes each student taking a turn to read a paragraph. Students record their clunks and gists for each paragraph in their Learning Logs. The teacher hears many good questions being asked: "What does 'barbarians' mean?" "Was Prometheus a person?" "Why did the Greeks think they were very special?" The group discussions seem to help students learn meaningful information on their own.

The teacher brings the class back together as a whole group and uses the Clunk Bug strategy with students' clunks that have definitions in the article. Students add their clunks to their Semantic Maps. Students explain which fix-up strategies were used to figure out the meaning of unknown words. Gists are recorded on sentence strips and posted for use with the "Wrap Up" strategy. Gists are evaluated according to the following criteria: must be a paraphrase, must be the most important information about the "who" or "what" that will help students remember the important details in the paragraph, and must be concise. Many teachers instruct students that their gists should not be longer than ten words. They call this "the ten finger guideline."

Wrap Up/Vocabulary

Most groups have very different Wrap Ups, which reflect the diversity and individuality of the students. Students refer back to their gist statements on the sentence strips and their Learning Logs to create a summary of their reading. Headings and subheadings of the article are turned into questions for students to answer. The teacher conducts Clunk Bug challenges to review the problematic vocabulary. Predictions are reviewed regarding their accuracy; students provide information they have learned from the article for their predictions.

Evaluation

Each group is responsible for answering one of the review questions for the article and sharing their answer with the class. The teacher administers the vocabulary test to conclude the lesson.

Conclusions

In this chapter, we have provided suggestions for adapting CSR for secondary level content area instruction. Secondary students who struggle with reading must learn effective strategies for tackling content area text. Instructional challenges are common, as noted in the "Glimpse From the Classroom" scenario that begins this chapter. Teachers can serve students well by working collaboratively to promote the integration of CSR into content area work. We have discussed some of the areas, such as teaming, materials, instructional grouping, and vocabulary instruction, where adaptations can be helpful for integrating CSR into instruction. We hope these ideas will help teachers address the challenges they face when working with struggling readers and provide these students with the learning strategies that will help them become more independent and successful learners.

References

Bryant, D. P., N. Ugel, S. Thompson, & A. Hamff. (1999). Strategies to promote content area reading instruction. *Intervention in School and Clinic*, *34*(5), 293–302.

Lenz, B. K., & C. A. Hughes. (1990). A word identification strategy for adolescents with learning disabilities. *Journal of Learning Disabilities*, *23*(3), 149–163.

Meyer, B. J. F., & G. E. Rice. (1984). The structure of text. In P. D. Pearson, R. Barr, M. L. Kamil, & P. Mosenthal (Eds.), *Handbook of Reading Research, Vol. I* (pp. 319–351). White Plains, NY: Longman.

Palincsar, A. S., & A. L. Brown. (1984). The reciprocal teaching of comprehension-fostering and comprehension-monitoring activities. *Cognition and Instruction*, *1*, 117–175.

Rivera, D. P., & D. D. Smith. (1997). *Teaching students with learning and behavior problems* (3rd ed.). Boston: Allyn & Bacon.

West, G. B. (1978). *Teaching reading skills in content areas: A practical guide to the construction of student exercises* (2nd ed.). Oviedo, FL: Sandpiper Press, Inc.

The PALS Series

K-PALS (Kindergarten Peer-Assisted Literacy Strategies)

Patricia G. Mathes, Ph.D.;
Jeannine Clancy-Menchetti, M.A.;
and Joseph K. Torgesen, Ph.D.

Grades PreK-K

Actively engage all your students in fun, research-validated literacy activities that double phonemic awareness and alphabetic knowledge practice without adding extra time to your current literacy program. Students are paired for activities, increasing early reading gains for all—even those at risk for reading failure. Each 20-minute session includes class and pair games that teach pronunciation, letter knowledge, and phonological and phonemic awareness. This unique 20-week program (three sessions per week) provides essential practice to mastery, ensuring a solid foundation in early reading skills. Included are detailed teacher training lessons, Daily Direction Cards, Student Game Sheets, and more!

Professional Development Available
212 pages, 144 reproducibles (1C156PALS)

First Grade PALS (Peer-Assisted Literacy Strategies)

Patricia G. Mathes, Ph.D.; Joseph K. Torgesen, Ph.D.; Shelley H. Allen, Ph.D.; and Jill Howard Allor, Ed.D.

Grades K-1

Enhance your current reading program, increase all your students' reading levels, and decrease your referrals of low-achieving students to special education classes with *First Grade PALS*. You'll be able to measure student progress and skill levels in phonological awareness, fluency, word identification, nonsense-word reading, comprehension, and more. *First Grade PALS* includes tasks all students can successfully perform, and it creates opportunities for lower-functioning students to assume an integral role in a valued activity.

The manual outlines a variety of teacher procedures, such as how to schedule a PALS session, pair your students, and prepare related materials. Included are project-related benefits, a time line, a detailed overview, Daily Direction Cards, Game Sheets, and blackline masters.

Professional Development Available
222 pages, 150 reproducibles (1C157PALS1)

Teacher-Directed PALS (Paths to Achieving Literacy Success)

Patricia G. Mathes, Ph.D.; Jill Howard Allor, Ed.D.; Joseph K. Torgesen, Ph.D.; and Shelley H. Allen, Ph.D.

Grades PreK-1

This supplemental program was created especially for paraprofessionals and parents to use with beginning or struggling readers. Through explicit instructional content, the program focuses on the critical elements and skills students need to increase their reading abilities. Two simple routines—Sounds and Words and Story Sharing—help students apply newly learned skills to reading connected text. The 57 Sounds and Words lessons consist of fast-paced activities like letter sounds, sight-word reading, hearing sounds, passage reading, and sounding out. Story Sharing uses pretend reading, reading aloud, and retelling to teach students how to strategically approach text.

Professional Development Available
276 pages (1C142TDP)

REWARDS

Reading Excellence: Word Attack and Rate Development Strategies

Anita L. Archer, Ph.D.;
Mary M. Gleason, Ph.D.; and
Vicky Vachon, Ph.D.

Grades 4–12

**The Multisyllabic Word
Reading Program**

Help struggling readers meet and surpass grade level expectancies! In this 20-lesson program, a flexible strategy is outlined that can move students from an early elementary reading level to one of increased fluency and comprehension.

Many students, while having mastered reading skills learned in first and second grades, become "stuck" on multisyllabic words, hindering their reading fluency and negatively affecting their ability to succeed in most subjects. The *REWARDS* method of "decoding" words by segmenting their parts is key to the creatively designed exercises in this program.

Students participating in this program will:
- Decode previously unfamiliar multisyllabic words containing two to eight parts.
- Accurately read more multisyllabic words within one sentence.
- Accurately read more multisyllabic words found in science, social studies, and other classroom materials.
- Read content-area passages accurately and fluently.
- Experience increased comprehension as their accuracy and fluency increase.

Field-tested with positive results in intensive remedial programs as well as in general and special education classes, this program can dramatically improve your students' reading abilities and the quality of their work in other subjects. It can also increase confidence levels.

Teaching should have its REWARDS!
The *Teacher's Guide* includes lessons and scripts, overhead masters, assessment tests, practice word lists, and more. Student materials are available in the consumable *Student Book*.

Professional Development Available
Teacher's Guide (382 pages), Student Book (84 pages)
Student Book Set (10 copies)

REWARDS Video

Pick up some pointers!

Anita Archer demonstrates her teaching methods in this 30-minute *REWARDS* video. Produced as a support tool for trainers, the VHS features Dr. Archer in an actual classroom setting as she leads her students through several *REWARDS* exercises. Though not a training video, you'll view techniques to keep children focused and gain insight on ways to derive the most benefit from the program. Witness real students developing skills that enable them to tackle those tough, multisyllabic words—and see, firsthand, why Anita Archer is the recipient of eight Outstanding Teacher awards.

REWARDS Video (1C136VID)

Together We Can!

ClassWide Peer Tutoring to Improve Basic Academic Skills

Charles Greenwood, Ph.D.;
Joseph Delquadri, Ph.D.;
and Judith Carta, Ph.D.

Grades 1–8

A Program of Juniper Gardens Children's Project

Drill and memorization become a fun part of the day, off-task behavior is reduced, and practice time increases when you implement this research-based, peer-tutoring program. Individual class members are competing teams. The result is significant academic gain in any content area that involves memorization and drill. Includes easy-to-follow directions, reproducible masters, and four 20" x 30" dry-erase charts.

Professional Development Available
81-page book and 4 dry-erase charts (1C95SET)